Seal of the State of New Mexico

CHRONOLOGY AND DOCUMENTARY HANDBOOK OF THE STATE OF NEW MEXICO

ROBERT I. VEXLER

State Editor

WILLIAM F. SWINDLER

Series Editor

1978 OCEANA PUBLICATIONS, INC./Dobbs Ferry, New York

HOUSTON PUBLIC LIBRARY

R01 0846 7840

Library of Congress Cataloging in Publication Data

Main entry under title:

Chronology and documentary handbook of the State of
   New Mexico.

   (Chronologies and documentary handbooks of the
States ; 31)
      Bibliography: p.
      Includes index.
      SUMMARY: A chronology of historical events in the
State of New Mexico with selected documents, biographi-
cal outlines of politicians and prominent personalities,
and a name index.
      1. New Mexico — History — Chronology.   2. New Mexico —
Biography.   3. New Mexico — History — Sources.
[1. New Mexico — History]   I. Vexler, Robert I.
II. Series.
F796.C43   978.9   78-64403
ISBN 0-379-16156-7

©Copyright 1978 by Oceana Publications, Inc.

All rights reserved. No part of this publication may be reproduced or transmitted in any
form or by any means, electronic or mechanical, including photocopy, recording,
xerography, or any information storage and retrieval system, without permission in
writing from the publisher.

Manufactured in the United States of America

TABLE OF CONTENTS

INTRODUCTION	ix
CHRONOLOGY (1534-1977)	1
BIOGRAPHICAL DIRECTORY	25
PROMINENT PERSONALITIES	35
FIRST STATE CONSTITUTION	39
SELECTED DOCUMENTS	73
Da Vaca's Journey to New Mexico	75
New Mexico's National Park	85
The People of New Mexico	90
New Mexico: Terrain and Wild Life	105
Reclaiming the Arid Southwest	132
Basic Facts	141
Map of Congressional Districts	143
SELECTED BIBLIOGRAPHY	147
NAME INDEX	149

ACKNOWLEDGMENT

Special recognition should be accorded Melvin Hecker, whose research has made a valuable contribution to this volume.

Thanks to my wife, Francine, in appreciation of her help in the preparation of this work.

Thanks also to my children, David and Melissa, without whose patience and understanding I would have been unable to devote the considerable time necessary for completing the state chronology series.

Robert I. Vexler

INTRODUCTION

This projected series of <u>Chronologies and Documentary Handbooks of the States</u> will ultimately comprise fifty separate volumes - one for each of the states of the Union. Each volume is intended to provide a concise ready reference of basic data on the state, and to serve as a starting point for more extended study as the individual user may require. Hopefully, it will be a guidebook for a better informed citizenry - students, civic and service organizations, professional and business personnel, and others.

The editorial plan for the <u>Handbook</u> series falls into six divisions: (1) a chronology of selected events in the history of the state; (2) a short biographical directory of the principal public officials, e.g., governors, Senators and Representatives; (3) a short biographical directory of prominent personalities of the state (for most states); (4) the first state constitution; (5) the text of some representative documents illustrating main currents in the political, economic, social or cultural history of the state; and (6) a selected bibliography for those seeking further or more detailed information. Most of the data found in the present volume, in fact, have been taken from one or another of these references.

The current constitutions of all fifty states, as well as the federal Constitution, are regularly kept up to date in the definitive collection maintained by the Legislative Drafting Research Fund of Columbia University and published by the publisher of the present series of <u>Handbooks</u>. These texts are available in most major libraries under the title, <u>Constitutions of the United States: National and State</u>, in two volumes, with a companion volume, the <u>Index Digest of State Constitutions</u>.

Finally, the complete collection of documents illustrative of the constitutional development of each state, from colonial or territorial status up to the current constitution as found in the Columbia University collection, is being prepared for publication in a multi-volume series by the present series editor. Whereas the present series of <u>Handbooks</u> is intended for a wide range of interested citizens, the series of annotated constitutional materials in the volumes of <u>Sources and Documents of U. S. Constitutions</u> is primarily for the specialist in government, history or law. This is not to suggest that the general citizenry may not profit equally from referring to these materials; rather, it points up the separate purpose of the <u>Handbooks</u>, which is to guide the user to these and other sources of authoritative information with which he may systematically enrich his knowledge of this state and its place in the American Union.

William F. Swindler
Series Editor

Robert I. Vexler
Series Associate Editor

Crescit Eundo/
It Grows As It Goes
State Motto

CHRONOLOGY

1534	Cabeza de Vaca, Doruntes, Castillo, and Esteban, a slave belonging to Doruntes, were able to escape from their Indian captors and travelled across New Mexico.
1539	Francisco Vasquez de Coronado explored New Mexico.
1540	April - July. Francisco Vasquez de Coronado again travelled through New Mexico. He set up his headquarters in the region during the winter of 1540-41.
1580	Francisco Chumuscado led an expedition to New Mexico. He died on the trip back.
1581	Fray Augustin Rodriguez, a Franciscan Friar, travelled through the valley of the Rio Grande.
1582-83	Antonio Espejo explored the territory east and west of the Rio Grande extensively.
1593-94	Francisco Leyva de Bonille and Antonio Gutierrez de Humana spent this year in the Pueblo country surrounding San Ildefonso.
1598	Spring. Juan de Onate founded the first Spanish settlement on the Rio Grande River after having taken possession of New Mexico. He and his 400 settlers had chosen a site 30 miles northwest of the present day Santa Fe. The settlement was renamed San Gabriel in 1599.
	December 4. Juan de Zaldivar, leading a group of 18 men, was attacked by Indians. 13 were killed.
1599	July 12. Spanish troops attacked the Acoma Indians, destroying their pueblo. Between 600 and 800 Indians were killed, and another 600 were taken captive.
1600	December 24. Reinforcements from Mexico reached Juan de Onate's camp.

1601   June. Between 70 and 100 men began their search for Quivira. They returned in November having been no more successful than Coronado.

1609   Don Pedro de Renalta, who was the first royal governor of New Mexico arrived in the territory.

        The Mission Supply Service was founded. It was reorganized in 1644.

1610   Spring. Sante Fe was established as the new capital of the province.

1612   Friar Ordonez took charge of the missions in New Mexico.

1625   Felipe de Sotelo became governor of the province and served until 1637.

1637   Luis de Rosas became governor of New Mexico and served in the office until 1641.

1642   Fall. Alonso Pacheco, the newly appointed governor of New Mexico arrived at Santa Fe. He served until 1656.

1656   Friar Thomas Manso was instrumental in having his brother named governor of the region. Manso served until 1659, having helped to keep peace.

1659   Bernardo Lopez de Mendizabel became governor of New Mexico. Various people accused him of mistreating the Indians, being irreligious and showing disrespect for the church. He died while in office in 1661.

1661   Don Diego de Penalosa became governor of the province and continued in the office until 1664.

1680	August 9. Pope led a general revolt of the Pueblo Indians in which more than 400 Spaniards were killed. The remainder suffered a siege of Santa Fe from August 15 to 21 and then fled south to a mission located near the present city of El Paso. Several groups arrived there between September 3 and 13.

November 5. Governor Otermin, heading an expedition, departed for the region around Santa Fe. Otermin abandoned the province in December. The attempt to recapture the area was determined a failure. |
| 1683 | Domingo Jironza Petriz de Cruzate became governor of New Mexico. He served in office until 1686, regaining the position in 1688 and continued until 1689. Pedro Peresos Poseda was governor from 1686-88. |
| 1688 | Governor Cruzate led a small group of soldiers north. They fought the Indians at Zia Pueblo.

Don Diego de Vargas was appointed Governor of New Mexico. |
1691	February 22. Governor Don Diego de Vargas arrived in El Paso.
1692	August 21. Governor Don Diego de Vargas left El Paso. He led troops up the Rio Grande River and was able to convince the Indians to surrender Santa Fe.
1693	September. Approximately 800 settlers set out with their livestock and possessions for Santa Fe.
1697	Don Pedro Cubero became governor of New Mexico. He died while in office in 1704.
1706	Albuquerque was founded.

1804	Copper mining began on a large scale in the deposits located at Santa Rita in the Southwestern part of the state.
1821	William Becknell, a trader, pioneered the Santa Fe Trail between New Mexico and Missouri.
1822	Francisco Javier Chavez became governor of New Mexico under the Mexican Republic.
	Antonio Vizcarra became governor of the province under the Republic of Mexico. He served until 1823.
1823	Francisco Javier Chavez became acting governor of New Mexico.
	Bartolome Vaca became governor of the province and served until 1825.
1824	New Mexico was joined with Chihuahua and Durango forming the state of Estado Interno del Norte.
1825	Antonio Nurbara became governor of New Mexico, in which post he served until 1827.
1827	Manuel Armijo was appointed governor of the area and served until 1828.
1828	Antonio Vizcarra served as acting governor of New Mexico under the Republic of Mexico.
	Gold was discovered in the Ortiz Mountains located between Albuquerque and Sante Fe.
	Jose Antonio Chavez became governor and served until 1831.
1831	Santiago Abreu was appointed governor of New Mexico by the Republic of Mexico in which position he remained until 1833.
1833	Las Vegas was established.

Francisco Sarracino became governor of the province under the Mexican Republic. He served until 1835 except for a brief period during 1834.

1834 Juan Rafael Ortiz was acting governor of New Mexico.

El Crepusculo de la Libertud (The Dawn of Liberty) was issued as the first Spanish-language newspaper at Santa Fe.

1835 Mariano Chavez served as acting governor of New Mexico.

Albino Perez became governor of the province and continued in the office until 1837.

1836 New Mexico was raised to the status of a department, remaining in this condition until it was granted to the United States by the Treaty of Guadelupe Hidalgo in 1848.

1837 July. The northern Pueblo Indians rose in revolt.

Jose Gonzalez became revolutionary governor or pretendant of New Mexico, remaining in the office until 1838.

1838 Manuel Armijo became governor of the department and served until 1846, except for certain periods during which acting governors regulated affairs.

1841 Antonio Sandova was acting governor of New Mexico.

Claiming that the Rio Grande River was its western boundary, the Republic of Texas sent 300 men to New Mexico to maintain its claims. The New Mexican militia captured the Texans and sent them to Mexico where they were imprisoned briefly and then released.

1844	Mariano Martinez de Lejanza became acting governor in which position he remained until 1845.
1845	Jose Chavez served as acting governor.
1846	Juan Bautista vigil y Alarid was acting governor of New Mexico.
	Spring. The Mexican War broke out between the United States and Mexico.
	August 18. Brigadier-General Stephen W. Kearney reached Santa Fe and was able to capture the town without any opposition. Kearney organized the civil government. Charles Bent became governor of New Mexico in which position he served until he was killed during the Mexican revolt on January 19, 1847.
1847	January. Some of the Mexican residents of Santa Fe rose up in revolt and killed Governor Charles Bent on January 14. Other Americans and Mexicans who had taken office were also killed. The uprising was soon suppressed.
	Donanciano Vigil became governor, continuing in the office until 1848.
	The _Santa Fe Republican_ began publication as the first English-language paper in the territory.
1848	John Marshall Washington was appointed governor of New Mexico in his capacity as commander of the Department. He served in this capacity until 1844.
	New Mexico tried to enter the Union, going on record as being opposed to slavery.
	Las Cruces was founded.

1849   John Nuroe became governor of the territory in his capacity as commander of the department. He served in the office until 1851.

A Baptist school was established at Santa Fe.

1850   Population: 61,547

May 25. New Mexican residents established their own state government in a special convention where a constitution was adopted prohibiting slavery. In addition the delegates set the boundaries of the state and applied for statehood. The constitution was ratified by the citizens who then proceeded to select state officials to conduct the affairs of the state.

September 9. The United States Congress established the Territory of New Mexico as part of the compromise of 1850.

December 13. Congress passed the necessary legislation providing for a territorial form of government which was formally begun on March 3, 1851.

1851   March 3. James S. Calhoun, an Indian agent, became the first governor of the Territory of New Mexico. He remained in office until 1852.

April 2. The leader of the Mescarelo Apaches signed a treaty with the United States government.

August 8. Bishop Jean Baptiste Lamy arrived at Santa Fe.

Several forts were established at this time, including Fort Defiance, located immediately across the present state of Arizona in Nevaho country.

1852

January 9. The following counties were created: Bernalillo, Dona Ana, Rio Arribu, San Miguel, Santa Fe, Socomo, Taos, and Valencia.

Bernalillo, with its seat at Albuquerque, was named for Bernal Diaz de Castillo who served with Cortez during the conquest of Mexico. Dona Ana, with Las Cruces as its seat, was named for the daughter of Col. Ana who was captured by the Apache Indians.

Rio Arribu has its seat at Tierra Amarilla. San Miguel, with Las Vegas as its seat, was named for Saint Michael, the Archangel who struck down the rebel Lucifer. Santa Fe has its seat at Santa Fe. Socomo has its county seat at Socomo.

Taos, with Taos as its seat, was named for the Taos Indian tribe. Valencia has its seat at Los Lunas and was named for Valencia, Spain.

E. V. Sumner, the military commander, served as acting governor. The secretary of the Territory, John Greiner, was acting governor.

William Carr Lane was appointed governor of the Territory and served in the office until 1853.

The Sisters of Loretta founded a girls' academy in Santa Fe at the urging of Bishop Lamy.

A group of Jicarilla Apache's who had been fired on by some soldiers without provocation. The Indians took revenge on troops and white settlers.

1853

December 30. The Gadsden Purchase was arranged whereby 45,535 square miles was added to the southern part of the Territory. President Franklin Pierce announced the acquisition on June 30, 1854.

CHRONOLOGY

David Meriwether became governor of the Territory and served in this capacity until 1857.

1854   March 30. Jicarilla led a Ute war party of 250 in an attack upon 60 cavalry men, killing 43 soldiers. The United States troops claimed they had killed 200 indians. Col. Philip St. George Cooke, commandant of Fort Union carried the struggle into Indian territory.

The first French priests reached Santa Fe.

1855   January. Captain Richard S. Ewell led a winter campaign into the Mescalero Apache country. Although the United States forces suffered from various ambushes, they were able to destroy many Indian villages. The Indians soon made pleas for peace.

Fort Stanton was established in Indian Territory.

1856   The territorial legislature passed a law which severely limited the rights of free blacks. They were encouraged by implication to leave the region.

1857   March. The United States congress passed a law providing economic aid the Overland Mail Route through the south, running through St. Louis and Memphis to Fort Smith, Arkansas thence westward through El Paso and Fort Yuma to Los Angeles, California.

Abraham Rencher became governor of New Mexico in which office he served until 1861.

1858   Commanche Indians attacked the white village on Red River 130 miles from Fort Union.

1859   The Brothers of the Christian Schools established St. Michael's High School and

College in Santa Fe.

The legislature passed a slave code for New Mexico.

Some purebred Merino sheep were brought into the territory from Kentucky.

1860 Population: 93,516.

February 1. Mora County, with its seat at More, was created.

1861 July 1. Captain John Robert Baylor, commanding a group of Texas cavalrymen, occupied Fort Bliss.

July 23. Captain Baylor left Fort Bliss and marched northward to occupy Mesilla.

July 25. Major Isaac Lynde led his Union troops toward Mesilla and demanded that the southern forces surrender. After the exchange of some shots the northern troops returned to Fort Fillmore. Shortly thereafter Major Lynde abandoned Fort Fillmore in a questionable and cowardly action. He went to Fort Stanton 154 miles Northeast.

Henry Connelly became Governor of the territory and served in the office until 1865.

Part of northeastern New Mexico was removed to form part of Colorado.

1862 January. Col. H. H. Sibley gathered an army of 3,800 Texans and entered New Mexico.

February. Col. H. H. Sibley and his Confederate troops sought and won a victory at Valverde on the Rio Grande River, defeating Col. Edward R. S. Canby. Sibley and his men occupied Albuquerque and Santa Fe.

March - April. Union troops drove Col. Sibley's Texan troops out of New Mexico.

Congress passed a law prohibiting slavery in New Mexico.

1863 All land West of the 109th meridian was placed in the Territory of Arizona.

Magdalena and Socomo were the first mining centers of silver.

General James H. Carleton began a campaign against the Navajoes who were eventually subdued and placed on a reservation on the Pecos River. They were later moved to the northwestern portion of the Territory.

1865 W. E. M. Asny, secretary of the Territory, became acting governor of New Mexico in which post he served until 1866.

1866 The Presbyterians started a school at Lagena Pueblo.

Robert B. Mitchell became governor of the Territory of New Mexico and served in the office until 1869.

Charles Goodnight and Oliver Loring began a trail for a cattle drive from Fort Belknap on the Brazos River going in a southwestward direction until it reached the Pecos River at Horsehead Crossing.

1867 March 2. Congress abolished the condition of peonage.

1868 A gold rush occurred near Toas.

January 30. Grant County was established with its seat at Silver City. It was named for Ulysses Simpson Grant, Major General in the United States Army during the Civil War, and later with President of United States.

General Sherman arranged a treaty with the Navajo Indians which provided for their return to the territory occupied by their ancestors. The Navajo reservation still exists in this area.

1869   January 16. Lincoln County, with its county seat at Carrizozo, was established. It was named for Abraham Lincoln, 16th President of the United States.

January 25. Colfax County, with Raton as its seat, was created. It was named for Schuyler Colfax, Vice President of the United States under President

William A. Pile became governor of the territory and served in the office until 1871.

1870   Population: 91,874

1871   Marsh Gidding became governor of New Mexico and served in this capacity until 1875.

1872   A state constitution was drafted. The state was to be called Lincoln, but the movrement did not gain many adherents.

The Denver and Rio Grande Railroad was constructed southward to Pueblo.

1873   December 1. A group of men led by the Horrell (Harrold or Howell) brothers shot up the town of Lincoln, killing the constable who tried to stop them.

One of the brothers and a friend were wounded, captured and shot in cold blood. The group had been driven out of Texas because of the cold blooded murders they committed and had come to Lincoln town in the spring of 1873. The Horrell's attacked a group of Mexican's at a wedding on December 20. They eventually returned to Texas.

The Mescalero Reservation was formally established.

1875   William G. Ritch, secretary of the Territory served as acting governor for a brief period.

Samuel B. Axtell Became governor of New Mexico and served in this capacity until 1878.

Alexander McSween came to Lincoln. He was a capable leader of the anti-Murphy Faction.

The New Mexico statehood bill failed to achieve the necessary two-thirds vote as a result of a misunderstanding concerning Stephen B. Elkin's stand on the issues involved in the rights of the southern states and the Force Bill.

1876   The Lincoln County War broke out, continuing until 1878. This struggle was a conflict between newly arrived settlers and long-time residents who had the law officers on their side.

1878   September. Lewis Wallace who had previously been appointed Governor of New Mexico, arrived in Santa Fe. He was able to help solve the difficulties in Lincoln County by requesting that the President declare martial law in the area. Wallace served as governor until 1881.

1879   March 6. Governor Wallace reached Lincoln.

The Apache chief Victorio led an uprising which was finally ended in 1880.

1880   Population: 119,565

1881   Lionel A. Sheldon became governor of the territory and served in the office until 1885

The Southern Pacific Railroad reached El Paso.

Sheriff Pat Garrett killed the outlaw Billy the Kid near Fort Sumter.

1884   April 3. Sierra County, with its seat at Truth or Consequences, was created.

1885   Edmund G. Ross became governor of New Mexico and continued to serve in this capacity until 1889.

Geronimo, the Apache chief, led an uprising which was finally subdued in 1886.

1887   February 27. San Juan County, with Aztec as its seat, was established. It was named for Saint John the Baptist.

1889   February 23. McKinley County, with Gallup as its county seat, was created. It was named for William McKinley, Representative from Ohio, governor of Ohio and 25th President of the United States from 1897 to 1901.

The territorial legislature established the University of New Mexico at Albuquerque. In addition a school of mines was founded at Socarro and an agricultural college at Las Cruces.

A Constitutional Convention adopted a constitution which was rejected when it was submitted to the voters.

L. Bradford Prince became governor of the territory and served until 1893.

February 25. Chaves and Eddy Counties were created. Chaves, with its seat at Carlsbud was named for Mariano Chaves. Eddy has its seat at New Rockford and was named for Charles B. Eddy who helped develop the Carlsbud irrigation project.

CHRONOLOGY

1890	Population: 160,282
1891	February 26. Guadelupe County, with its seat at Santa Rosa, was created. It was named for Guadalupe Hidalgo, the city and federal district in Mexico and for the Guadalupe River.
	The town of Gallup was incorporated. Roswell was also incorporated as a village.
	The New Mexico Military Institute was founded.
1893	February 23. Union County, with Clayton as its seat, was established.
	William T. Thornton became governor of the territory and served in the office until 1897.
	The town of Carlsbad was founded.
1897	Miguel A. Otero became governor of New Mexico and served in this capacity until 1906.
	The Santa Fe Railroad took over the bankrupt Atlantic and Pacific Railroad.
1898	The town of Almagordo was founded as a railroad division point.
	The Rock Island Railroad entered New Mexico.
1899	January 30. Otero County, with its seat at Almagordo, was established. It was named for Miguel Antonio Otero, governor and la- later treasurer of New Mexico.
1900	Population: 195,310.
1901	May. President William McKinley stopped at Deming while en route to the west coast.

1903   February 28. Quay and Roosevelt Counties were established. Quay, with its seat at Tucomcari, was named for Matthew Stanley Quay, member of the Pennsylvania House of Representatives and Senator from Pennsylvania. Roosevelt, with Portales as its county seat, was named for Theodore Roosevelt, governor of New York, Vice President and 26th President of the United States.

March 10. Sandoval County, with Bernalillo as its seat, was established. It was named for the Sandoval family.

March 16. Torrance County, with its seat at Estancia, was created. It was named for Francis Torrance, the promoter of the New Mexico Central Railroad.

1906   November 6. A referendum proposing the joint admission of New Mexico and Arizona as a single state with the name of Arizona. The voters of New Mexico approved of the venture, but the residents of Arizona rejected it.

Herbert J. Hagerman became governor of the territory and served during the year.

1907   J. W. Reynolds, secretary of the territory, served as acting governor of New Mexico.

George Curry became governor of New Mexico and served in this capacity until 1909.

Clovis was established as a division point of the Santa Fe Railroad.

1908   Livingston was founded.

1909   February 25. Curry County, with its seat at Clovis, was established. It was named for George Curry, a lieutenant and captain in Theodore Roosevelt's Rough Riders during the Spanish American War and governor of

New Mexico Territory.

William J. Mills served as governor of New Mexico

1910   Population: 327,301.

June 20. The United States Senate passed a bill whilc would enable New Mexico and Arizona to form state constitutions and state governments. President William Howard Taft signed the bill into law.

1911   August 18. The Flood statehood resolution was passed providing for the admission of New Mexico and Arizona as states.

1912   January 6. New Mexico was admitted to the Union as the 47th state.

William C. McDonald, Democrat, who had been elected in 1911, became first governor of the state of New Mexico. He served in the office until January 1, 1917.

1913   February 3. The state legislature ratified the 16th Amendment to the United States Constitution.

March 13. The state legislature ratified the 17th Amendment to the United States Constitution.

1914   The Santa Fe Railroad constructed a segment of the road between Galveston and Clovis which linked New Mexico with the Gulf of Mexico.

1916   March 9. The Mexican bandit Pancho Villa raided Columbus, killing 17 persons. General John J. Pershing was ordered to lead United States troops in an invasion of Mexico on March 15 in order to stop Villa.

May 9. President Woodrow Wilson ordered the Militia of Texas, New Mexico and Arizona mobilized to serve on the Mexican border as a result of difficulties with Mexico.

Elephant Butte Dam was completed.

1917 January 1. Ezequiel Cabeza de Baca, Democrat, who had been elected in 1916, became governor of the state. He served briefly until his death on February 18, 1917.

February 18. Lieutenant Governor Washington E. Lindsey, a Roosevelt Progressive, became governor of the state. He served until the end of the term on January 1, 1919

February 28. De Baco County, with its seat at Fort Sumner, was created. It was named for Ezequiel Cabeza de Baca, second governor of the state.

March 7. Lea County, with Lovington as its seat, was established. It was named for Joseph C. Lea, a pioneer of New Mexico.

1919 January 1. Octaviano A. Larrazola, Republican who had been elected in 1918, became governor of the state. He served in the office until the end of his term on January 1, 1921.

January 20. The state legislature ratified the 18th Amendment to the United States Constitution.

February 25. Hidalgo County, with its seat at Lordsburg, was created. It was named for Guadalupe Hidalgo, Mexico.

1920 Population: 360,350

February 21. Governor Larrazola approved the ratification of the 19th Amendment to the United States Constitution, which had been previously ratified by the state legislature.

1921

January 1. Merritt C. Mechem, Republican, who had been elected in 1920, became governor of the state and served in the office until the end of his term on January 1, 1923.

February 25. Catron County, with its seat at Reserve, was created. It was named for Thomas Benton Catron, who served in the Confederate Army during the Civil War, was a member of the territorial council, delegate to the Unites States Congress and United States Sentor from New Mexico.

March 4. Harding County, with its seat at Mosquero, was established. It was named for William Gamaliel Harding, Senator from Ohio and 29th President of the United States.

1922

Station KOB began broadcasting at Albuquerque as the first radio station in the state.

Geologists discovered oil in the southeastern and northwestern parts of the state.

1923

January 1. James J. Hinley, Democrat, who had been elected in 1922, became governor of the state. He served in the post until January 1, 1925.

Carlsbad Caverns National Park was created with 46, 756 acres.

1925

January 1. Arthur T. Hannett, Democrat, who had been elected in 1924, became governor of New Mexico and served until January 1, 1927.

A geologist searching for oil accidentally found potash near Carlsbud.

1927   January 1. Richard C. Dillan, Republican, who had been elected in 1926, became governor of the state and served for two terms until January 1, 1931.

1930   Population: 423,317.

1931   January 1. Arthur Seligman, Democrat, who had been elected in 1930, became governor of New Mexico and served in the office until his death on September 24, 1933.

1933   January 21. The state legislature ratified the 20th Amendment to the United States Constitution.

September 25. Lieutenant Governor Andrew W. Hockenhull, Democrat, became governor of the state upon the death of Arthur Seligman. Hockenhull served in the office until the end of the term on January 1, 1935.

November 2. The state legislature ratified the 21st Amendment to the United States Constitution.

1935   January 1. Clyde Tingley, Democrat, who had been elected in 1934, became governor of the state and served in the office until January 1, 1939.

1939   January 1. John E. Miles, Democrat, became governor of New Mexico and served until January 1, 1943.

1940   Population: 531,818

1942   Los Alamos was selected as the national center for nuclear research. It had been a ranch school for boys.

1945　　　　June 2. Clinton P. Anderson was appointed secretary of Agriculture by President Harry S. Truman. Anderson assumed his office on June 30, 1945.

July 16. The first atomic bomb was successfully tested near Alamogardo.

1947　　　　January 1. Thomas J. Mabry, Democrat, who had been elected in 1946, became governor of the state and served until January 1, 1951.

1948　　　　Station KOB-TV began broadcasting at Albuquerque as the first television station in the state.

March 16. Los Alamos County was established with its seat at Los Alamos.

1950　　　　Population: 681,187

Spring. Paddy Martinez, a Navajo Indian, discovered uranium in the northwestern part of the state.

1951　　　　January 1. Edwin L. Mechem, Republican, who had been elected in 1950, became governor of the state and served in the office until January 1, 1955, having been re-elected in 1952.

February 12. The state legislature ratified the 22nd Amendment to the United States Constitution.

1955　　　　January 1. John F. Simms, Democrat, who had been elected in 1954, became governor of New Mexico and served in the post until January 1, 1957.

1957　　　　January 1. Edwin L. Mechem, Republican, who had been elected in 1956, became governor of the state and served in the office until January 1, 1959.

1959   January 1. John Burroughs, Democrat, who had been elected in 1958, became governor of the state and served in the post until January 1, 1961.

1960   Population: 951,023.

Farmington was founded.

1961   January 1. Edwin L. Mechem, Republican, who had been elected in 1960, again became governor of the state and served in the office until his resignation on November 30. 1962.

February 1. The state legislature ratified the 23rd Amendment to the United States Constitution.

1962   June 13. President John F. Kennedy signed a bill which authorized two water projects in New Mexico: The Navajo Indian project and the San Juan-Chama project which was to carry water from the western to the eastern slopes of the Rocky Mountains.

November 30. Lieutenant Governor Tom Bolack, Republican, became governor of New Mexico upon the resignation of Edwin L. Mechem.

1963   January 1. Jack M. Campbell, Democrat, who had been elected in 1962, became governor of New Mexico and served in the office until January 1, 1967.

March 5. The state legislature ratified the 24th Amendment to the United States Constitution.

1964   Construction of the San Juan-Chama project began in order to bring water through the Rocky Mountains to the region around Albuquerque.

1965	June 17-26. The Arkansas and South Platte River's flooded, killing two people.
1966	February 3. The state legislature ratified the 25th Amendment to the United States Constitution.
1967	January 1. David F. Cargo, Republican, who had been elected in 1966, became governor of the state and served until January 1, 1971.
1969	The state legislature passed a bill which was signed by Governor Cargo, abolishing the death penalty.
1970	Population: 1,016,000
1971	January 1. Bruce King, Democrat, who had been elected in 1970, became governor of the state and served in this capacity until January 1, 1975.
1972	July 17. The United States government offered the Navajo Indian tribe full control of all Bureau of Indian Affairs operations in the Reservation which was located in the states of Arizona, New Mexico and Utah.
1973	February 12. The state legislature ratified the Equal Rights Amendment to the United States Constitution.
1975	January 1. Jerry Apodaca, Democrat, became governor of New Mexico.
	March 13. The Fairchild Camera and Instrument Corporation announced the permanent closing of its Shiprock, N. Mex. electronics plant. It had been occupied for eight days by armed members of the American Indian Movement, protesting the layoff of 140 Indian workers.

April 18. The United States Nuclear Regulatory Commission approved the export of 1.4 million pounds of uranium for processing in Great Britain and the Soviet Union. It was taken from mines in Wyoming and New Mexico.

November 11. Former Senator Anderson died.

1976 September 7. The Democratic Vice Presidential nominee, Walter Mondale, visited Albuquerque.

September 18. Democratic Presidential nominee Jimmy Carter visited Albuquerque on a campaign tour.

October 27. Republican Vice Presidential nominee Dole attended a political rally in Albuquerque.

1977 June 16-22. A forest fire burned up 12,000 acres of New Mexican northern and central timberland.

BIOGRAPHICAL DIRECTORY

The selected list of governors, United States Senators and Members of the House of Representatives for New Mexico, 1861-1977, includes all persons listed in the Chronology for whom basic biographical data was readily available. Older biographical sources are frequently in conflict on certain individuals, and in such cases the source most commonly cited by later authorities was preferred.

ANDERSON, Clinton Presba
    Democrat
    b. Centerville, S. Dak., October 23, 1895
    U. S. Representative, 1941-45
    U. S. Secretary of Agriculture, 1945-48
    U. S. Senator, 1949-

ANDREWS, William Henry
    Republican
    b. Youngsville, Pa., January 14, 1846
    d. Carlsbad, N. Mex., January 16, 1919
    U. S. Representative (Territorial Delegate),
        1905-12

APODACA, Jerry
    Democrat
    b. Las Cruces, N. Mex., October 3, 1934
    Governor of New Mexico, 1975-

BOLAND, Tom
    Republican
    Governor of New Mexico, 1962-63

BRATTON, Sam Gilbert
    Democrat
    b. Kosse, Texas, August 19, 1848
    d. Albuquerque, N. Mex., September 22,
        1963
    U. S. Senator, 1925-33

BURROUGHS, John
    Democrat
    Governor of New Mexico, 1959-61

BURSOM, Holm Olaf
    Republican
    b. Fort Dodge, Iowa, February 10, 1867
    d. Colorado Springs, Colo., August 7,
        1953
    U. S. Senator, 1921-25

CAMPBELL, Jack M.
    Democrat
    b. Hutchinson, Kansas, September 10,
        1916
    Governor of New Mexico, 1963-67

CARGO, David Francis
    b. Dowagiac, Mich., January 13, 1929

Governor of New Mexico, 1967-71

CATRON, Thomas Benton
    Republican
    b. near Lexington, Mo., October 6, 1840
    d. Santa Fe, N. Mex., May 15, 1921
    U. S. Representative (Territorial Delegate),
        1895-97
    U. S. Senator, 1912-17

CHAVES, Jose Francisco
    Republican
    b. Padillas, Mexico (now New Mexico),
        June 27, 1833
    d. by assassination at Pinoswells (near
        Cedarville(, N. Mex., November 26,
        1904
    U. S. Representative (Territorial Delegate),
        1865-67; Representative, 1869-71

CHAVEZ, Dennis
    Democrat
    b. Los Chavez, N. Mex., April 8, 1888
    d. Washington, D. C., November 18, 1962
    U. S. Representative, 1931-35
    U. S. Senator, 1935-62

CLEVER, Charles P.
    Democrat
    b. Cologne, Prussia, February 23, 1830
    d. Tome, N. Mex., July 8, 1874
    U. S. Representative (Territorial Delegate),
        1867-69

CURRY, George
    Republican
    b. Greenwood plantation, near Bayou Sara,
        La., April 3, 1863
    d. Albuquerque, N. Mex., November 27, 1947
    Governor of the Territory of New Mexico,
        1907-11
    U. S. Representative, 1912-13

CUTTING, Bronson Murray
    Republican
    b. Oakdale, Long Island, N. Y., June
        23, 1888
    d. in an airplane crash near Atlanta, Mo.,
        May 6, 1935
    U. S. Senator, 1927-28, 1929-35

DE BACA, Ezequiel C.
    Democrat
    Governor of New Mexico, 1917

DEMPSEY, John Joseph
    Democrat
    b. White Haven, Pa., June 22, 1879
    d. Washington, D. C., March 11, 1958
    U. S. Representative, 1935-41
    Governor of New Mexico, 1943-47
    U. S. Representative, 1951-58

DILLON, Richard Charles
    Republican
    b. St. Louis, Mo., June 24, 1877
    d. January 4, 1966
    Governor of New Mexico, 1927-31

ELKINS, Stephen Benton
    Republican (New Mexico - West Virginia)
    b. Perry County, Ohio, September 26, 1841
    d. Washington, D. C., January 4, 1911
    U. S. Representative (Territorial Delegate-
        New Mexico), 1873-77
    U. S. Senator (New Mexico), 1895-1911
    U. S. Secretary of War, 1891-93

FALL, Albert Bacon
    Republican
    b. Frankfort, Ky., November 26, 1861
    d. El Paso, Texas, November 30, 1944
    U. S. Senator, 1912-21
    U. S. Secretary of the Interior, 1921-23

FERGUSSON, Harvey Butler
    Democrat
    b. near Pickensville, Ala., September 9,
        1848
    d. Albuquerque, N. Mex., June 10, 1915
    U. S. Representative (Territorial Delegate),
        1897-99; (Representative), 1912-15

GALLEGOS, Joel Manuel
    Democrat
    b. in what is now Rio Arriba County, N. Mex.,
        October 30, 1815
    d. Santa Fe, N. Mex., April 21, 1875
    U. S. Representative (Territorial Delegate),
        1853-56, 1871-73

HANNETT, Arthur Thomas
    b. Lyons, N. Y., February 17, 1884
    Governor of New Mexico, 1925-27

HATCH, Carl Atwood
    Democrat
    b. Kirwin, Kans., November 27, 1889

NEW MEXICO

    d. Albuquerque, N. Mex., September 12, 1963
    U. S. Senator, 1933-49

HERNANDEZ, Benigno Cardenas
    Republican
    b. Tais, N. Mex., February 13, 1862
    d. Los Angeles, Calif., October 18, 1954
    U. S. Representative, 1915-17, 1919-21

HINKLE, James Fielding
    Democrat
    b. Franklin County, Mo., October 20, 1864
    d. March 26, 1951
    Governor of New Mexico, 1923-25

HOCKENHULL, Andrew W.
    Democrat
    Governor of New Mexico, 1933-35

JONES, Andreius Aristieus
    Democrat
    b. near Union City, Tenn., May 16, 1862
    d. Washington, D. C., December 20, 1927
    U. S. Senator, 1917-27

JOSEPH, Antonio
    Democrat
    b. Taos, N. Mex., August 25, 1846
    d. Ojo Caliente, N. Mex., April 19, 1910
    U. S. Representative (Territorial Delegate),
        1885-95

KING, Bruce
    Democrat
    b. Stanley, N. Mex., April 6, 1924
    Governor of New Mexico, 1971-75

LARRAZOLO, Octaviano Ambrosio
    Republican
    b. Allende, State of Chihuahua, Mexico,
        December 7, 1859
    d. Albuquerque, N. Mex., April 7, 1930
    Governor of New Mexico, 1919-21
    U. S. Senator, 1928-29

LINDSAY, Washington Ellsworth
    Republican
    b. Belmont County, Ohio, December 29, 1862
    d. April 5, 1926
    Governor of New Mexico, 1917-19

LUJAN, Manue, Jr.
    Republican

b. on a farm near the Indian Pueblo of
   San Ildefonso, N. Mex., May 12, 1928
U. S. Representative, 1969-

LUNA, Tranquillino
   Republican
   b. Los Lunas, N. Mex., February 25, 1849
   d. Peralta, N. Mex., November 20, 1892
   U. S. Representative (Territorial Delegate),
      1881-84

LUSK, Georgia Lee
   Democrat
   b. Carlsbad, N. Mex., May 12, 1893
   d. Albuquerque, N. Mex., January 5, 1971
   U. S. Representative, 1947-49

MABRY, Thomas J.
   Governor of New Mexico, 1947-51

MCDONALD, William C.
   b. Jordanville, N. Y., July 25, 1858
   d. April 11, 1918
   Governor of New Mexico, 1912-17

MANZANARES, Francisco Antonio
   Democrat
   b. Abiquia, N. Mex., January 25, 1843
   d. Las Vegas, N. Mex., September 17, 1904
   U. S. Representative (Territorial Delegate),
      1884-85

MECHEM, Edwin Leard
   Republican
   b. Alamogardo, N. Mex., July 2, 1912
   Governor of New Mexico, 1951-54, 1957-58,
      1961-62
   U. S. Senator, 1962-64

MECHEM, Merritt Cramer
   b. Ottawa, Kansas, October 10, 1870
   d. ----
   Governor of New Mexico, 1921-23

MILES, John Esten
   Democrat
   b. Murfreesboro, Tenn., July 28, 1884
   d. ----
   Governor of New Mexico, 1939-42
   U. S. Representative, 1949-51

MONTOYA, Joseph Manuel
   Democrat

b. Penablanca, N. Mex., September 24, 1915
U. S. Representative, 1957-64
U. S. Senator, 1964-

MONTOYA, Nestor
  Republican
  b. Old Albuquerque, N. Mex., April 14, 1862
  d. Washington, D. C., January 13, 1923
  U. S. Representative, 1921-23

MORRIS, Thomas Gayle
  Democrat
  b. Eastland County, Texas, August 20, 1919
  U. S. Representative, 1959-69

MORROW, John
  Democrat
  b. near Darlington, Wis., April 19, 1865
  d. Santa Fe, N. Mex., February 25, 1935
  U. S. Representative, 1923-29

OTERO, Mariano Sabino
  Republican
  b. Peratta, N. Mex., August 29, 1844
  d. Albuquerque, N. Mex., February 1, 1904
  U. S. Representative (Territorial Delegate),
     1879-81

OTERO, Miguel Antonio
  Democrat
  b. Valencia, N. Mex., June 21, 1829
  d. Las Vegas, N. Mex., May 30, 1882
  U. S. Representative (Territorial Delegate),
     1856-61

PEREA, Francisco
  Republican
  b. Los Padillas, N. Mex., January 9, 1830
  d. Albuquerque, N. Mex., May 21, 1913
  U. S. Representative (Territorial Delegate),
     1863-65

PEREA, Pedro
  Republican
  b. Bernalillo, N. Mex., April 22, 1852
  d. Bernalillo, N. Mex., January 11, 1906
  U. S. Representative (Territorial Delegate),
     1899-1901

RODEY, Bernard Shandon
  Republican
  b. County Mayo, Ireland, March 1, 1856

d. Albuquerque, N. Mex., March 10, 1927
U. S. Representative (Territorial Delegate),
   1901-05

ROMERO, Trinidad
   Republican
   b. Santa Fe, N. Mex. (then Part of Mexico),
      June 15, 1835
   d. Las Vegas, N. Mex., August 28, 1918
   U. S. Representative (Territorial Delegate),
      1877-79

SELIGMAN, Arthur
   Democrat
   b. Santa Fe, N. Mex., June 14, 1873
   d. September 25, 1933
   Governor of New Mexico, 1931-33

SIMMS, Albert Gallatin
   Republican
   b. Washington, Ark., October 8, 1882
   d. Albuquerque, N. Mex., December 29, 1964
   U. S. Representative, 1929-33

SIMMS, John F.
   Democrat
   Governor of New Mexico, 1955-57

TINGLEY, Clyde
   Democrat
   b. London, Ohio, January 5, 1883
   d. December 24, 1960
   Governor of New Mexico, 1935-39

WALKER, E. S. Johnny
   Democrat
   b. Fulton, Ky., June 18, 1911
   U. S. Representative, 1965-69

WALTON, William Bell
   Democrat
   b. Altoona, Pa., January 23, 1871
   d. Silver City, N. Mex., April 14, 1939
   U. S. Representative, 1917-19

WATTS, John Sebrie
   Republican
   b. Boone County, Ky., January 19, 1816
   d. Bloomington, Ind., June 11, 1876
   U. S. Representative (Territorial Delegate),
      1861-63

WEIGHTMAN, Richard Hanson
    Democrat
    b. Washington, D. C., December 28, 1816
    d. on the battlefield at Wilson Creek, Mo.,
       August 10, 1861
    U. S. Representative (Territorial Delegate),
       1851-53

PROMINENT PERSONALITIES

The following select list of prominent persons of New Mexico has been selected to indicate the valuable contributions they have made to American life.

BONNEY, William H. ("Billy the Kid"
    b. New York, N. Y., November 23, 1859
    d. when fatally shot by Sheriff Pat F.
       Garrett, Fort Sumter, N. Mex.,
       July 15, 1881
    1871 - said to have killed first man
    1876 - Billy and companion killed
       three Indians - beginning his "career"

BLUMENSHEIN, Ernest L.
    b. 1874
    d. 1960
    Illustrator for Century, Scribner's
       McClure's, Harper's, American and other
       magazines and books, 1896-1908
    Chiefly portrait work since 1908.

CONDON, Edward U.
    b. Alamagordo, N. Mex., 1902
    Associate Professor of Physics, Princeton
       University, 1930-37
    Associate Director Westinghouse Research
       Laboratories, 1937-45
    Member government uranium committees, 1941-43
    Director, U. S. Bureau of Standards, 1945-

DA ANZA, Juan Bautista
    b. 1735
    d. 1788
    Explored California route
    Founded San Francisco, 1775
    Governor of New Mexico, 1777-87
    Established Colorado River colonies, 1780

OTERO, Miguel Antonio
    b. St. Louis, Mo., October 17, 1789
    d. August 7, 1944
    Governor of Territory of New Mexico, 1897-
       1906
    Treasurer of New Mexico, 1909-11
    U. S. Marshal for District of Canal Zone,
       Isthmus of Panama, 1917-21
    Author: Conquistadores of Spain and Buccaneers
       of England, France and Holland, 1925.
          The Real Billy the Kid with New Light
       on the Lincoln County War, 1935.
          My Memoirs, 1882 to 1897, 1935.
          My Nine Years as Governor of the
       Territory of New Mexico, 1897-1906, 1936.

PRINCE, L. Bradford
    b. Flushing, N. Y., 1840
    d. December 7, 1922
    Member New York Assembly, 1871-75
    Member New York Senate, 1876-77
    Chief Justice of the Territory of New
        Mexico, 1879-82
    Governor of Territory of New Mexico, 1889-93

VARGAS, Diego de
    b. c. 1650
    d. April 4, 1704
    Engaged in suppressing Indian uprisings,
        1693-97
    Appointed Governor of New Mexico, 1696
    Governor of New Mexico, 1701-03

FIRST STATE CONSTITUTION

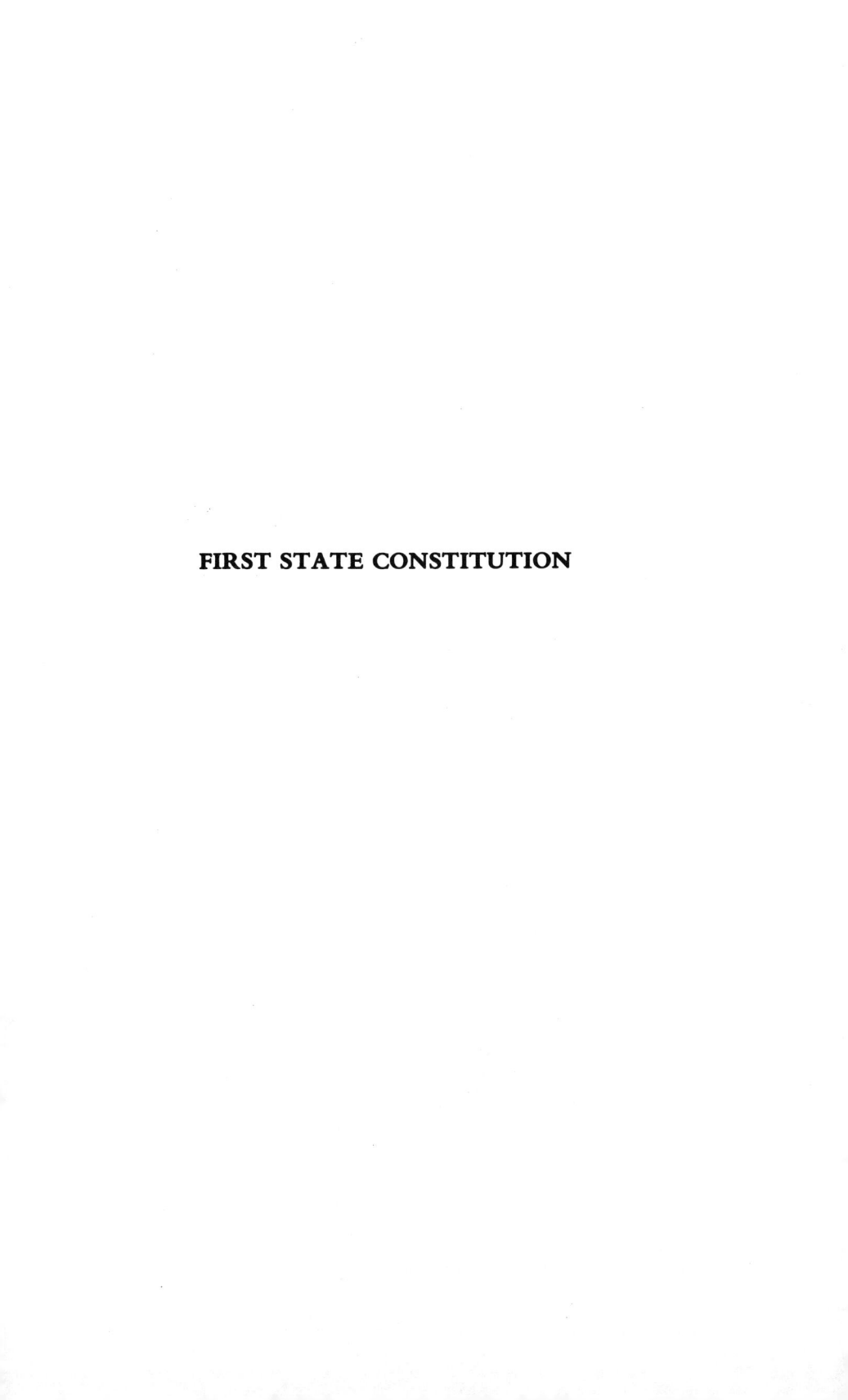

FIRST STATE CONSTITUTION

Constitution of 1910·
1912[1]

[PREAMBLE]

We, the people of New Mexico, grateful to Almighty God for the blessings of liberty, in order to secure the advantages of a State government, do ordain and establish this Constitution.

ARTICLE I
NAME AND BOUNDARIES

The name of this State is New Mexico, and its boundaries are as follows:

Beginning at a point where the thirty-seventh parallel of north latitude intersects the one hundred and third meridian west from Greenwich; thence along said one hundred and third meridian to the thirty-second parallel of north latitude; thence along said thirty-second parallel to the Rio Grande; also known as the Rio Bravo del Norte, as it existed on the ninth day of September, one thousand eight hundred and fifty; thence following the main channel of said river, as it existed on the ninth day of September, one thousand eight hundred and fifty, to the parallel of thirty-one degrees forty-seven minutes north latitude; thence west one hundred miles to a point; thence south to the parallel of thirty-one degrees twenty minutes north latitude; thence along said parallel of thirty-one degrees twenty minutes, to the thirty-second meridian of longitude west from Washington; thence along said thirty-second meridian to the thirty-seventh parallel of north latitude; thence along said thirty-seventh parallel to the point of beginning.

---

[1] Framed by a constitutional convention which met at Santa Fe, New Mexico, from October 3, 1910 until November 21, 1910, and ratified by the voters on January 21, 1911. The joint resolution of Congress admitting New Mexico as a state in the Union was conditioned on the adoption of an amendment to the article providing for amendments. This amendment was adopted at the following State election (November 5), and on January 6, 1912, the President issued his proclamation by which New Mexico was admitted as a state, and on that day the Constitution became effective.

ARTICLE II
BILL OF RIGHTS

Section 1. [Supreme law of the land] The State of New Mexico is an inseparable part of the Federal Union, and the Constitution of the United States is the supreme law of the land.

Sec. 2. [Popular sovereignty] All political power is vested in and derived from the people; all government of right originates with the people, is founded upon their good will and is instituted solely for their good.

Sec. 3. [Right of self government] The people of the State have the sole and exclusive right to govern themselves as a free, sovereign and independent State.

Sec. 4. [Inherent rights] All persons are born equally free, and have certain natural, inherent and inalienable rights, among which are the rights of enjoying and defending life and liberty, of acquiring, possessing and protecting property, and of seeking and obtaining safety and happiness.

Sec. 5. [Treaty rights] The rights, privileges and immunities, civil, political and religious, guaranteed to the people of New Mexico by the treaty of Guadalupe Hidalgo shall be preserved inviolate.

Sec. 6. [Right to bear arms] The people have the right to bear arms for their security and defense, but nothing herein shall be held to permit the carrying of concealed weapons.

Sec. 7. [Habeas corpus] The privilege of the writ of habeas corpus shall never be suspended, unless, in case of rebellion or invasion, the public safety requires it.

Sec. 8. [Freedom of elections] All elections shall be free and open, and no power, civil or military, shall at any time interfere to prevent the free exercise of the right of suffrage.

Sec. 9. [Military power subordinate] The military shall always be in strict subordination to the civil power; no soldier shall in time of peace be quartered in any house without the consent of the owner, nor in time of war except in the manner prescribed by law.

Sec. 10. [Searches and seizures] The people shall be secure in their persons, papers, homes and effects, from unreasonable searches and seizures, and no warrant to search any place, or seize any person or thing, shall issue without describing the place to be searched, or the persons or things to be seized, nor without a written showing of probable cause, supported by oath or affirmation.

Sec. 11. [Freedom of religion] Every man shall be free to worship God according to the dictates of his own conscience, and no person shall ever be molested or denied any civil or political right or privilege on account of his religious opinion or mode of religious worship. No person shall be required to attend any place of worship or support any religious sect or denomination; nor shall any preference be given by law to any religious denomination or mode of worship.

Sec. 12. [Trial by jury] The right of trial by jury as it has heretofore existed shall be secured to all and remain inviolate. In all cases triable in courts inferior to the District Court the jury may consist of six. The Legislature may provide that verdicts in civil cases may be rendered by less than a unanimous vote of the jury.

Sec. 13. [Bail] All persons shall be bailable by sufficient sureties, except for capital offenses, when the proof is evident or the presumption great. Excessive bail shall not be required, nor excessive fines imposed, nor cruel and unusual punishment inflicted.

Sec. 14. [Indictment] No person shall be held to answer for a capital, felonious or infamous crime unless on a presentment or indictment of a grand jury or information filed by a district attorney or Attorney-General or their deputies, except in cases arising in the militia when in actual service in time of war or public danger. No person shall be so held on information without having had a preliminary examination before an examining magistrate, or having waived such preliminary examination.

[Grand jury] A grand jury shall be composed of such number, not less than twelve, as may be prescribed by law. Citizens only, residing in the county for which a grand jury may be convened and qualified as prescribed by law, may serve on a grand jury. Concurrence necessary for the finding of an indictment by a grand jury shall be prescribed by law; provided: such concurrence shall never be by less than a majority of those who compose a grand jury and provided at least eight must concur in finding an indictment when a grand jury is composed of twelve in number. Until otherwise prescribed by law a grand jury shall be composed of twelve in number of which eight must concur in finding an indictment. A grand jury shall be convened upon order of a judge of a court empowered to try and determine cases of capital, felonious or infamous crimes at such times as to him shall be deemed necessary, or a grand jury shall be ordered to convene by such judge upon the filing of a petition therefor signed by not less than seventy-five resident taxpayers of the county, or a grand jury may be convened in any additional manner as may be prescribed by law.

[Rights of accused] In all criminal prosecutions, the accused shall have the right to appear and defend himself in person, and by counsel; to demand the nature and cause of the accusation; to be confronted with the witness against him; to have the charge and testimony interpreted to him in a language that he understands; to have compulsory process to compel the attendance of necessary witnesses in his behalf, and a speedy public trial by an impartial jury of the county or district in which the offense is alleged to have been committed.[2]

Sec. 15. [Self incrimination—double jeopardy] No person shall be compelled to testify against himself in a criminal proceeding, nor shall any person be twice put in jeopardy for the same offense; and when the indictment, information or affidavit upon which any person is convicted charges different offenses or different degrees of the same offense and a new trial is granted the accused, he may not again be tried for an offense or degree of the offense

[2] As amended November 4, 1924. New Mexico Laws, 1923, p. 351.

greater than the one of which he was convicted.

Sec. 16. [Treason] Treason against the State shall consist only in levying war against it, adhering to its enemies, or giving them aid or comfort. No person shall be convicted of treason unless on the testimony of two witnesses to the same overt act, or on confession in open court.

Sec. 17. [Freedom of speech and press] Every person may freely speak, write and publish his sentiments on all subjects, being responsible for the abuse of that right; and no law shall be passed to restrain or abridge the liberty of speech or of the press. In all criminal prosecutions for libels, the truth may be given in evidence to the jury; and if it shall appear to the jury that the matter charged as libelous is true and was published with good motives and for justifiable ends, the party shall be acquitted.

Sec. 18. [Life, liberty, property] No person shall be deprived of life, liberty or property without due process of law; nor shall any person be denied the equal protection of the laws.

Sec. 19. [Retroactive laws] No ex-post facto law, bill of attainder, nor law impairing the obligation of contracts shall be enacted by the Legislature.

Sec. 20. [Eminent domain] Private property shall not be taken or damaged for public use without just compensation.

Sec. 21. [Imprisonment for debt] No person shall be imprisoned for debt in any civil action.

Sec. 22. [Alien land-ownership] Until otherwise provided by law no alien ineligible to citizenship under the laws of the United States, or corporation, co-partnership or association, a majority of the stock or interest in which is owned or held by such aliens, shall acquire title, leasehold or other interest in or to real estate in New Mexico.[3]

Sec. 23. [Reserved rights] The enumeration in this Constitution of certain rights shall not be construed to deny, impair or disparage others retained by the people.

[3] As amended November 7, 1922. New Mexico Laws, 1921, p. 469.

ARTICLE III
DISTRIBUTION OF POWERS

Section 1. [Separation of powers] The powers of the government of this State are divided into three distinct departments, the Legislative, Executive and Judicial, and no person or collection of persons charged with the exercise of powers properly belonging to one of these departments, shall exercise any powers properly belonging to either of the others, except as in this Constitution otherwise expressly directed or permitted.

ARTICLE IV
LEGISLATIVE DEPARTMENT

Section 1. [Legislature] The legislative power shall be invested in a Senate and House of Representatives which shall be designated the Legislature of the State of New Mexico, and shall hold its sessions at the seat of government.

[Referendum] The people reserve the power to disapprove, suspend and annul any law enacted by the Legislature, except general appropriation laws; laws providing for the preservation of the public peace, health or safety; for the payment of the public debt or interest thereon, or the creation of funding of the same, except as in the Constitution otherwise provided; for the maintenance of the public schools or State institutions, and local or special laws. Petitions disapproving any law other than those above excepted, enacted at the last preceding session of the Legislature, shall be filed with the Secretary of State not less than four months prior to the next general election. Such petitions shall be signed by not less than ten per centum of the qualified electors of each of three-fourths of the counties and in the aggregate by not less than ten per centum of the qualified electors of the State, as shown by the total number of votes cast at the last preceding general election. The question of the approval or rejection of such law shall be submitted by the Secretary of State to the electorate at the next general election; and if a majority of the legal votes cast thereon, and not less than forty per centum of the total number of legal votes cast at such general election, be cast for the rejection of such law, it shall be annulled and thereby repealed with the same effect as if the Legislature had then repealed it, and such repeal shall revive any laws repealed by the act so annulled; otherwise it shall remain in force unless subsequently repealed by the Legislature. If such petition or petitions be signed by not less than twenty-five per centum of the qualified electors under each of the foregoing conditions, and be filed with the Secretary of State within ninety days after the adjournment of the session of the Legislature at which such laws were enacted, the operation thereof shall be thereupon suspended and the question of its approval or rejection shall be likewise submitted to a vote at the next ensuing general election. If a majority of the votes cast thereon and not less than forty per centum of the total number of votes cast at such general election be cast for its rejection, it shall be thereby annulled; otherwise it shall go into effect upon publication of the certificate of the Secretary of State declaring the result of the vote thereon. It shall be a felony for any person to sign any such petition with any name other than his own, or to sign his name more than once for the same measure, or to sign such petition when he is not a qualified elector in the county specified in such petition; provided, that nothing herein shall be construed to prohibit the writing thereon of the name of any person who cannot write and who signs the same with his mark. The Legislature shall enact laws necessary for the effective exercise of the power hereby reserved.

Sec. 2. [Legislative powers] In addition to the powers herein enumerated, the Legislature shall have all powers necessary to the Legislature of a free State.

Sec. 3. [Qualifications of legislators] The Senate shall consist of twenty-four, and the House of Representatives of forty-nine members, who shall be qualified electors of their respective districts and residents of New Mexico for at least three years next preceding their election. Senators shall not be less than twenty-five years, and representatives not less than twenty-one years of age at the time of their election. No person shall be eligible to the Legislature who, at the time of qualifying, holds any office of trust or profit under the State, county or national government, except notaries public and officers of the militia who receive no salary.

Sec. 4. [Election of legislators] Members of the Legislature shall be elected as follows: Senators for the term of four years, and members of the House of Representatives for the term of two years. They shall be elected on the day provided by law for holding the general election of State officers or representatives in Congress. Vacancies in either house shall be filled by an election at a time to be designated by the Governor.

Sec. 5. [Sessions] The first session of the Legislature shall begin at twelve o'clock, noon, on the day specified in the proclamation of the Governor. Subsequent sessions shall begin at twelve o'clock, noon, on the second Tuesday of January next after each general election. No regular session shall exceed sixty days, except the first which may be ninety days, and no special session shall exceed thirty days.

Sec. 6. [Special sessions] Special sessions of the Legislature may be called by the Governor, but no business shall be transacted except such as relates to the objects specified in his proclamation.

Sec. 7. [Powers of each house] Each House shall be the judge of election and qualifications of its own members. A majority of either House shall constitute a quorum to do business, but a less number may effect a temporary organization, adjourn from day to day, and compel the attendance of absent members.

Sec. 8. [Officers of the legislature] The Senate shall be called to order in the hall of the Senate by the Lieutenant-Governor. The Senate shall elect a president pro-tempore who shall preside in the absence of the Lieutenant-Governor and shall serve until the next session of the Legislature. The House of Representatives shall be called to order in the hall of said House by the Secretary of State. He shall preside until the election of a speaker, who shall be the member receiving the highest number of votes for that office.

Sec. 9. [Salaries of legislative officers] The Legislature shall choose its own officers and employees and fix their compensation, but the number and compensation shall never exceed the following: For each House, one chaplain, at three dollars per day; one chief clerk and one sergeant-at-arms, each at six dollars per day; one assistant chief clerk and one assistant sergeant-at-arms, each at five dollars per day; two enrolling clerks and two reading clerks, each at five dollars per day; six stenographers for the Senate and eight for the House, each at six dollars per day; and such subordinate employes in addition to the above as they may require, but the aggregate compensation of such additional employes shall not exceed twenty dollars per day for the Senate and thirty dollars per day for the House.

Sec. 10. [Compensation of legislators] Each member of the Legislature shall receive as compensation for his services the sum of five dollars for each day's attendance during each session and ten cents for each mile traveled in going to and returning from the seat of government by the usual traveled route, once each session, and he shall receive no other compensations, perquisite or allowance.

Sec. 11. [Parliamentary rules] Each House may determine the rules of its procedure, punish its members or others for contempt or disorderly behavior in its presence, and protect its members against violence; may, with the concurrence of two-thirds of its members, expel a member, but not a second time for the same act. Punishment for contempt or disorderly behavior or by expulsion shall not be a bar to criminal prosecution.

Sec. 12. [Public sessions—journal] All sessions of each House shall be public. Each House shall keep a journal of its proceedings, and the yeas and nays on any question shall, at the request of one-fifth of the members present, be entered thereon. The original thereof shall be filed with the Secretary of State at the close of the session, and shall be printed and published under his authority.

Sec. 13. [Privileges of legislators] Members of the Legislature shall, in all cases except treason, felony and breach of the peace, be privileged from arrest during their attendance at the session of their respective Houses, and on going to and returning from the same. And they shall not be questioned in any other place for any speech or debate or for any vote cast in either House.

Sec. 14. [Adjournments] Neither House shall, without the consent of the other, adjourn for more than three days, Sunday excepted; nor to any other place than that where the two Houses are sitting; and on the day of the final adjournment they shall adjourn at twelve o'clock noon.

Sec. 15. [Bills—enacting clause—readings] No law shall be passed except by bill, and no bill shall be so altered or amended on its passage through either House as to change its original purpose. The enacting clause of all bills shall be: "Be it enacted by the Legislature of the State of New Mexico." Any bill may originate in either House. No bill, except bills to provide for the public peace, health and safety, and codification or revision of the laws, shall become a law unless it has been printed, and read three different times in each House, not more than two of which readings shall be on the same day, and the third of which shall be in full.

Sec. 16. [Title—appropriation bills] The subject of every bill shall be clearly expressed in its title, and no bill embracing more than one subject shall be passed except general appropriation bills and bills for the codification or revision of the laws; but if any subject is embraced in any act which is not expressed in its title, only so much of the act which is not so expressed shall be void. General appropriation bills shall embrace nothing but appropriations for the expense of the executive, legislative and judiciary departments, interest, sinking fund, payments on the public debt, public schools, and other expenses required by existing laws; but if any such bill contains any other matter, only so much thereof as is hereby forbidden to be placed therein shall be void. All other appropriations shall be made by separate bills.

Sec. 17. [Passage of bills] No bill shall be passed except by a vote of a majority of the members present in each House, nor unless on its final passage a vote be taken by yeas and nays, and entered on the journal.

Sec. 18. [Amendment by reference] No law shall be revised or amended, or the provisions thereof extended by reference to its title only; but each section thereof as revised, amended or extended shall be set out in full.

Sec. 19. [Time limits for introduction of bills] No bill shall be introduced at any regular session of the Legislature subsequent to the forty-fifth legislative day, except the general appropriation bill, bills to provide for the current expenses of the government, and such bills as may be referred to the Legislature by the Governor by special message specifically setting forth the emergency or necessity requiring such legislation.[4]

Sec. 20. [Enrollment—signing of bills] Immediately after the passage of any bill or resolution, it shall be enrolled and engrossed, and read publicly in full in each House, and thereupon shall be signed by the presiding officer of each House in open session, and the fact of such reading and signing shall be entered on the journal. No interlineation or erasure in a signed bill, shall be effective, unless certified thereon in express terms by the presiding officer of each House quoting the words interlined or erased, nor unless the fact of the making of such interlineation or erasure be publicly announced in each House and entered on the journal.

Sec. 21. [Alteration or theft of bills] Any person who shall, without lawful authority, materially change or alter, or make away with, any bill pending in or passed by the Legislature, shall be deemed guilty of a felony and upon conviction thereof shall be punished by imprisonment in the penitentiary for not less than one year nor more than five years.

Sec. 22. [Veto] Every bill passed by the Legislature shall, before it becomes a law, be presented to the Governor for approval. If he approve, he shall sign it, and deposit it with the Secretary of State; otherwise, he shall return it to the house in which it originated, with his objections which shall be entered at large upon the journal; and such bill shall not become a law unless thereafter approved by two-thirds of the members present and voting in each house by yea and nay vote entered upon its journal. Any bill not returned by the Governor within three days, Sundays excepted, after being presented to him, shall become a law, whether signed by him or not, unless the Legislature by adjournment prevent such return. Every bill presented to the Governor during the last three days of the session shall be approved or disapproved by him within six days after the adjournment, and shall be by him immediately deposited with the Secretary of State. Unless so approved and signed by him such bill shall not become a law. The Governor may in like manner approve or disapprove any part or parts, item or items, of any bill appropriating money, and such parts or items approved shall become a law, and such as are disapproved shall be void, unless passed over his veto, as herein provided.

Sec. 23. [Date laws take effect] Laws shall go into effect ninety days after the adjournment of the Legislature enacting them, except general appropriation laws, which shall go into effect immediately upon their passage and approval. Any act necessary for the preservation of the public peace, health or safety, shall take effect immediately upon its passage and approval, provided it be passed by two-thirds of each house and such necessity be stated in a separate section.

Sec. 24. [Local or special laws] The Legislature shall not pass local or special laws in any of the following cases: Regulating county, precinct or district affairs; the jurisdiction and duties of justices of the peace, police magistrates and constables; the practice in courts of justice; the rate of interest on money; the punishment for crimes and misdemeanors; the assessment or collection of taxes or extending the time of collection thereof; the summoning or empanelling of jurors; the management of public schools; the sale or mortgaging of real estate of minors or others under disability; the change of venue in civil or criminal cases. Nor in the following cases: Granting divorces; laying out, opening, altering or working roads or highways, except as to State roads extending into more than one county, and military roads; vacating roads; town plats, streets, alleys or public grounds; locating or changing county seats, or changing county lines, except in creating new counties, incorporating cities, towns or villages or changing or amending the charter of any city, town or village; the opening or

---

[4] As amended November 8, 1932. New Mexico Laws, 1931, p. 303.

conducting of any election or designating the place of voting; declaring any person of age; chartering or. licensing ferries, toll bridges, toll roads, banks, insurance companies, or loan or trust companies; remitting fines, penalties, forfeitures or taxes; or refunding money paid into the State Treasury, or relinquishing, extending or extinguishing, in whole or in part, any indebtedness or liability of any person or corporation, to the State or any municipality therein; creating or decreasing fees, percentages or allowances of public officers; changing the laws of descent; granting to any corporation, association or individual the right to lay down railroad tracks or any special or exclusive privilege, immunity or franchise, or amending existing charters for such purpose; changing the rules of evidence in any trial or inquiry; the limitation of actions; giving effect to any informal or invalid deed, will or other instrument; exempting property from taxation; restoring to citizenship any person convicted of an infamous crime; the adoption or legitimizing of children; changing the name of persons or places; and the creation, extension or impairment of liens. In every other case where a general law can be made applicable, no special laws shall be enacted.

Sec. 25. [Laws validating official acts] No law shall be enacted legalizing the unauthorized or invalid act of any officer, remitting any fine, penalty or judgment against any officer, or validating any illegal use of public funds.

Sec. 26. [Special franchises] The Legislature shall not grant to any corporation or person, any rights, franchises, privileges, immunities or exemptions, which shall not, upon the same terms and under like conditions, inure equally to all persons or corporations; no exclusive right, franchise, privilege or immunity shall be granted by the Legislature or any municipality in this State.

Sec. 27. [Extra compensation] No law shall be enacted giving any extra compensation to any public officer, servant, agent or contractor after services are rendered or contract made; nor shall the compensation of any office be increased or diminished during his term of office, except as otherwise provided in this Constitution.

Sec. 28. [Appointment to new offices] No member of the Legislature shall, during the term for which he was elected, be appointed to any civil office in the State nor shall he within one year thereafter be appointed to any civil office created or the emoluments of which were increased during such term; nor shall any member of the Legislature during the term for which he was elected nor within one year, thereafter, be interested directly or indirectly in any contract with the State or any municipality thereof, which was authorized by any law passed during such term.

Sec. 29. [Laws creating debts] No law authorizing indebtedness shall be enacted which does not provide for levying a tax sufficient to pay the interest, and for the payment at maturity of the principal.

Sec. 30. [Payments of public money] Except interest or other payments on the public debt, money shall be paid out of the Treasury only upon appropriations made by the Legislature. No money shall be paid therefrom except upon warrant drawn by the proper officer. Every law making an appropriation shall distinctly specify the sum appropriated and the object to which it is to be applied.

Sec. 31. [Aid to private charities] No appropriation shall be made for charitable, educational or other benevolent purpose to any person, corporation, association or community not under the absolute control of the State, but the Legislature may, in its discretion, make appropriations for the charitable institutions and hospitals for the maintenance of which annual appropriations were made by the Legislative Assembly of nineteen hundred and nine.

Sec. 32. [Remission of debts to state] No obligation or liability of any person, association or corporation, held or owned by or owing to the State, or any municipal corporation therein, shall ever be exchanged, transferred, remitted, released, postponed, or in any way diminished by the Legislature, nor shall any such obligation or liability be extinguished except by the payment thereof into the proper treasury, or by proper proceeding in court.

Sec. 33. [Effect of repeal of law] No person shall be exempt from prosecution and punishment for any crime or offense against any law of this State by reason of the subsequent repeal of such law.

Sec. 34. [Change of judicial procedure] No act of the Legislature shall affect the right or remedy of either party, or change the rules of evidence or procedure, in any pending case.

Sec. 35. [Impeachment] The sole power of impeachment shall be vested in the House of Representatives, and a concurrence of a majority of all the members elected shall be necessary to the proper exercise thereof. All impeachments shall be tried by the Senate. When sitting for that purpose the senators shall be under oath or affirmation to do justice according to the law and the evidence. When the Governor or Lieutenant-Governor is on trial, the chief justice of the Supreme Court shall preside. No person shall be convicted without the concurrence of two-thirds of the senators elected.

Sec. 36. [Impeachable officers — penalty] All state officers and judges of the district court shall be liable to impeachment for crimes, misdemeanors and malfeasance in office, but judgment in such cases shall not extend further than removal from office and disqualification to hold any office of honor, trust or profit, or to vote under the laws of this State; but such officer or judge, whether convicted or acquitted, shall, nevertheless, be liable to prosecution, trial, judgment, punishment or civil action according to law. No officer shall exercise any powers or duties of his office after notice of his impeachment is served upon him until he is acquitted.

Sec. 37. [Passes] It shall not be lawful for a member of the Legislature to use a pass, or to purchase or receive transportation over any railroad upon terms not open to the general public; and the violation of this section shall work a forfeiture of the office.

Sec. 38. [Monopolies] The Legislature shall enact laws to prevent trusts, monopolies and combinations in restraint of trade.

Sec. 39. [Bribery] Any member of the Legislature who shall vote or use his influence for or against any matter pending in either house in consideration of any money, thing of value, or promise thereof, shall be deemed guilty of bribery; and any member of the Legislature or other person who shall directly or indirectly offer, give or promise any money, thing of value, privilege or personal advantage, to any member of the Legislature to influence him to vote or work for or against any matter pending in either house; or any member of the Legislature who shall solicit from any person or corporation any money, thing of value or personal advantage for his vote or influence as such member, shall be deemed guilty of solicitation of bribery.

Sec. 40. [Punishment for bribery] Any person convicted of any of the offenses mentioned in sections thirty-seven and thirty-nine hereof, shall be deemed guilty of a felony and upon conviction shall be punished by fine of not more than one thousand dollars or by imprisonment in the penitentiary for not less than one nor more than five years.

Sec. 41. [Testimony in bribery cases] Any person may be compelled to testify in any lawful investigation or judicial proceeding against another charged with bribery or solicitation of bribery as defined herein, and shall not be permitted to withhold his testimony on the ground that it might incriminate or subject him to public infamy; but such testimony shall not be used against him in any judicial proceeding against him except for perjury in giving such testimony.

APPORTIONMENT

Until changed by law as hereinafter provided, the legislative districts of the State shall be constituted as follows.

SENATORIAL DISTRICTS

First. The county of San Miguel, one senator.

Second. The counties of San Miguel and Mora, one senator to be a resident of Mora county and to be elected by the electors of Mora and San Miguel counties.

Third. The counties of Guadalupe and San Miguel, one senator.

Fourth. The county of Rio Arriba, one senator.

Fifth. The counties of Bernalillo, San Juan and Sandoval, one senator.

Sixth. The counties of Rio Arriba and Sandoval, one senator.

Seventh. The county of Bernalillo, one senator.

Eighth. The county of Colfax, one senator.
Ninth. The counties of Union and Colfax, one senator, to be a resident of Union county, and to be elected by the qualified electors of Union and Colfax counties.
Tenth. The county of Santa Fe, one senator.
Eleventh. The county of Taos, one senator.
Twelfth. The county of Valencia, one senator.
Thirteenth. The counties of Sierra, Grant, Luna and Socorro, one senator.
Fourteenth. The county of Socorro, one senator.
Fifteenth. The counties of Torrance, Otero, Lincoln, and Socorro, one senator.
Sixteenth. The county of Dona Ana, one senator.
Seventeenth. The county of McKinley, one senator.
Eighteenth. The counties of Otero and Lincoln, one senator.
Nineteenth. The county of Chaves, one senator.
Twentieth. The county of Eddy, one senator.
Twenty-first. The county of Roosevelt, one senator.
Twenty-second. The county of Quay, one senator,
Twenty-third. The county of Curry, one senator.
Twenty-fourth. The county of Grant, one senator.

REPRESENTATIVE DISTRICTS

First. The county of Valencia, two members.
Second. The county of Socorro, two members.
Third. The county of Bernalillo, three members.
Fourth. The county of Santa Fe, two members.
Fifth. The county of Rio Arriba, two members.
Sixth. The county of San Miguel, three members.
Seventh. The county of Mora, two members.
Eighth. The county of Colfax, two members.
Ninth. The county of Taos, two members.
Tenth. The county of Sandoval, one member.
Eleventh. The county of Union, two members.
Twelfth. The county of Torrance, one member.
Thirteenth. The county of Guadalupe, one member.

Fourteenth. The county of McKinley, two members.
Fifteenth. The county of Dona Ana, two members.
Sixteenth. The county of Lincoln, one member.
Seventeenth. The county of Otero, one member.
Eighteenth. The county of Chaves, three members.
Nineteenth. The county of Eddy, two members.
Twentieth. The county of Roosevelt, one member.
Twenty-first. The county of Luna, one member.
Twenty-second. The county of Grant, two members.
Twenty-third. The county of Sierra, one member.
Twenty-fourth. The county of San Juan, one member.
Twenty-fifth. The county of Quay, two members.
Twenty-sixth. The county of Curry, one member.
Twenty-seventh. The counties of Rio Arriba and Sandoval, one member.
Twenty-eighth. The counties of Torrance, Santa Fe and Guadalupe, one member.
Twenty-ninth. The counties of San Miguel and Guadalupe, one member.
Thirtieth. The counties of Lincoln, Otero and Socorro, one member.

Upon the creation of any new county it shall be annexed to some contiguous district for legislative purposes.

At its first session after the publication of the census of the United States in the year nineteen hundred and twenty and at the first session after each United States census thereafter, the Legislature may reapportion the legislative districts of the State upon the basis of population; provided, that each county included in each district shall be contiguous to some other county therein.

ARTICLE V

EXECUTIVE DEPARTMENT

Section 1. [Executive officers] The executive department shall consist of a Governor,

Lieutenant-Governor, Secretary of State, State Auditor, State Treasurer, Attorney-General, Superintendent of Public Instruction and Commissioner [of [a]] Public Lands, who shall be elected for the term of two years beginning on the first day of January next after their election.

Such officers shall, after having served two consecutive terms, be ineligible to hold any State office for two years thereafter.

The officers of the executive department, except the Lieutenant-Governor, shall, during their terms of office, reside and keep the public records, books, papers and seals of office at the seat of government.[b]

Sec. 2. [Election of state officers] The returns of every election for State officers shall be sealed up and transmitted to the Secretary of State, who, with the Governor and Chief Justice, shall constitute the State canvassing board which shall canvass and declare the result of the election. The person having the highest number of votes for any office, as shown by said returns, shall be declared duly elected. If two or more have an equal and the highest number of votes for the same office, one of them shall be chosen therefor by the Legislature on joint ballot.

Sec. 3. [Qualifications of officers] No person shall be eligible to any office specified in section one, hereof, unless he be a citizen of the United States, at least thirty years of age, nor unless he shall have resided continuously in New Mexico for five years next preceding his election; nor to the office of Attorney-General, unless he be a licensed attorney of the Supreme Court of New Mexico in good standing; nor to the office of superintendent of public instruction unless he be a trained and experienced educator.

Sec. 4. [Governor] The Supreme Executive power of the State shall be vested in the Governor, who shall take care that the laws be faithfully executed. He shall be commander-in-chief of the military forces of the State, except when they are called into the service of the United States. He shall have power to call out the militia to preserve the public peace,

---
[a] The enrolled copy reads "or."
[b] As amended November 3, 1914. New Mexico Laws, 1913, p. 175.

execute the laws, suppress insurrection and repel invasion.

Sec. 5. [To appoint officers] The Governor shall nominate, and, by and with the consent of the Senate, appoint all officers whose appointment or election is not otherwise provided for, and may remove any officer appointed by him for incompetency, neglect of duty or malfeasance in office. Should a vacancy occur in any State office, except Lieutenant-Governor and member of the Legislature, the Governor shall fill such office by appointment, and such appointee shall hold office until the next general election, when his successor shall be chosen for the unexpired term.

Sec. 6. [To pardon] Subject to such regulations as may be prescribed by law, the Governor shall have power to grant reprieves and pardons after conviction for all offenses except treason and in cases of impeachment.

Sec. 7. [Succession to governorship] In case of a vacancy in the office of Governor, the Lieutenant-Governor shall succeed to that office, and to the powers, duties and emoluments thereof. In case the Governor is absent from the State, or is for any reason unable to perform his duties, the Lieutenant-Governor shall act as Governor, with all the powers, duties and emoluments of that office until such disability is removed. In case there is no Lieutenant-Governor, or in case he is for any reason unable to perform the duties of Governor, then the Secretary of State, or, in case there is no Secretary of State, or he is for any reason unable to perform the duties of Governor, then the president pro tempore of the Senate shall succeed to the office of Governor, or act as Governor as hereinbefore provided.

Sec. 8. [President of senate] The Lieutenant Governor shall be president of the Senate, but shall vote only when the Senate is equally divided.

Sec. 9. [Public accounts] Each officer of the executive department and of the public institutions of the State shall keep an account of all moneys received by him and make reports thereof to the Governor under oath, annually, and at such other times as the Governor may require, and shall, at least thirty days preceding each regular session of the Legislature, make a full and complete report to the Governor, who shall transmit the same to the Legislature.

Sec. 10. [Seal] There shall be a State seal which shall be called the "Great Seal of the State of New Mexico," and shall be kept by the Secretary of State.

Sec. 11. [Commissions] All commissions shall issue in the name of the State, be signed by the Governor, and attested by the Secretary of State, who shall affix the State seal thereto.

Sec. 12. [Compensation of officers] The annual compensation to be paid to the officers mentioned in section one of this article shall be as follows: Governor, five thousand dollars; Secretary of State, three thousand dollars; State Auditor, three thousand dollars; State Treasurer, three thousand dollars; Attorney-General, four thousand dollars; Superintendent of Public Instruction, three thousand dollars, and Commissioner of Public Lands, three thousand dollars; which compensation shall be paid to the respective officers in equal quarterly payments.

The Lieutenant-Governor shall receive ten dollars per diem while acting as presiding officer of the Senate, and mileage at the same rate as a State senator.

The compensation herein fixed shall be full payment for all services rendered by said officers and they shall receive no other fees or compensation whatsoever.

The compensation of any of said officers may be increased or decreased by law after the expiration of ten years from the date of the admission of New Mexico as a State.

Sec. 13. [Residence of officers] All district, county, precinct and municipal officers shall be residents of the political subdivisions for which they are elected or appointed.

ARTICLE VI
JUDICIAL DEPARTMENT

Section 1. [Courts] The judicial power of the State shall be vested in the Senate when sitting as a court of impeachment, a Supreme Court, District Courts, Probate Courts, justices of the peace, and such courts inferior to the District Courts as may be established by law from time to time in any county or municipality of the State, including Juvenile Courts.

Sec. 2. [Appellate jurisdiction of supreme court] The Appellate Jurisdiction of the Supreme Court shall be co-extensive with the State; and shall extend to all final judgments and decisions of the District Courts, and said court shall have such appellate jurisdiction of interlocutory orders and decisions of the District Courts as may be conferred by law.

Sec. 3. [Original jurisdiction of supreme court] The Supreme Court shall have original jurisdiction in quo warranto and mandamus against all State officers, boards and commissions, and shall have a superintending control over all inferior courts; it shall also have power to issue writs of mandamus, error, prohibition, habeas corpus, certiorari, injunction and all other writs necessary or proper for the complete exercise of its jurisdiction, and to hear and determine the same. Such writs may be issued by direction of the court, or by any justice thereof. Each justice shall have power to issue writs of habeas corpus upon petition by or on behalf of a person held in actual custody, and to make such writs returnable before himself or before the Supreme Court, or before any of the District Courts or any judge thereof.

Sec. 4. [Election of supreme court] The Supreme Court of the State shall consist of three justices, who shall be elected at the general election for Representatives in Congress for a term of eight years.

At the first election for State officers after the adoption of this Constitution, there shall be elected three justices of the Supreme Court, who shall immediately qualify and classify themselves by lot, so that one of them shall hold office until four years, one until six years, and one until eight years from and after the first day of January, nineteen hundred and thirteen. A certificate of such classification shall be filed in the office of the Secretary of State. Until otherwise provided by law, the justice who has the shortest term to serve shall be the chief justice and shall preside at all sessions of the courts; and in his absence the justice who has the next shortest term shall preside; but no justice appointed or elected to fill a vacancy shall be chief justice.

Sec. 5. [Quorum] A majority of the justices of the Supreme Court shall be necessary to constitute a quorum for the transaction of business, and a majority of the justices must concur in any judgment of the court.

Sec. 6. [Absence of one justice] When a justice of the Supreme Court shall be interested in any case, or be absent, or incapacitated, the remaining justices of the court may, in their discretion, call in any district judge of the State to act as justice of the court.

Sec. 7. [Terms of court] The Supreme Court shall hold one term each year, commencing on the second Wednesday in January, and shall be at all times in session at the seat of government, provided, that the court may, from time to time, take such recess as in its judgment may be proper.

Sec. 8. [Qualifications of supreme justices] No person shall be qualified to hold the office of justice of the Supreme Court unless he be at least thirty years old, learned in the law, and shall have been in the actual practice of law and resided in this State or Territory, of New Mexico for at least three years. Any person whose time of service upon the bench of any District Court of this State or Territory of New Mexico, added to the time he may have practiced law, as aforesaid, shall be equal to three years, shall be qualified without having practiced for the full three years.

Sec. 9. [Officers of supreme court] The Supreme Court may appoint and remove at pleasure its reporter, bailiff, clerk, and such other officers and assistants as may be prescribed by law.

Sec. 10. [Increase in size of supreme court] After the publication of the census of the United States, in the year nineteen hundred and twenty, the Legislature shall have power to increase the number of justices of the Supreme Court to five; provided, however, that no more than two of said justices shall be elected at one time, except to fill a vacancy.

Sec. 11. [Compensation of supreme justices] The justices of the Supreme Court shall each receive an annual salary of six thousand dollars, payable quarterly.

Sec. 12. [Judicial districts] The State shall be divided into eight judicial districts, and a judge shall be chosen for each district by the qualified electors thereof at the election for representatives in Congress. The terms of office of the district judges shall be six years.

Sec. 13. [Jurisdiction of district courts] The District Court shall have original jurisdiction in all matters and causes not excepted in this Constitution, and such jurisdiction of special cases and proceedings as may be conferred by law, and appellate jurisdiction of all cases originating in inferior courts and tribunals in their respective districts and supervisory control over same. The District Courts, or any judge thereof shall have power to issue writs of habeas corpus, mandamus, injunction, quo warranto, certiorari, prohibition, and all other writs, remedial or otherwise in the exercise of their jurisdiction; provided, that no such writs shall issue directed to judges of courts of equal or superior jurisdiction. The District Courts also shall have the power of naturalization in accordance with the laws of the United States. Until otherwise provided by law, at least two terms of the District Court shall be held annually in each county, at the county seat.

Sec. 14. [Qualifications of district judges] The qualifications of the district judges sh ll be the same as those of justices of the Supreme Court. Each district judge shall reside in the district for which he was elected.

Sec. 15. [Transfer of district judges] Any district judge may hold District Court in any county at the request of the judge of such district.

Whenever the public business may require, the chief justice of the Supreme Court shall designate any district judge of the State to hold court in any district, and two or more district judges may sit in any district or county separately at the same time. If any judge shall be disqualified from hearing any cause in the district, the parties to such cause, or their attorneys of record, may select some member of the bar to hear and determine said cause, and act as judge pro tempore therein.

Sec. 16. [Increase in number of district judges] The Legislature may increase the number of district judges in any judicial district, and they shall be elected as other district judges. At its first session after the publication of the census of the United States in the year nineteen hundred and twenty, and at the first session after each United States census thereafter, the Legislature may rearrange the districts of the State, increase the number thereof, and make provision for a district judge for any additional district.

Sec. 17. [Compensation of district judges] Each judge of the District Court shall receive an annual salary of four thousand five hundred dollars, payable quarterly by the State.

Sec. 18. [Disqualifications of judges] No judge of any court nor justice of the peace shall, except by consent of all parties, sit in the trial of any cause in which either of the parties shall be related to him by affinity or consanguinity within the degree of first cousin, or in which he was counsel, or in the trial of which he presided in any inferior court, or in which he has an interest.

Sec. 19. [Judges ineligible to other offices] No judge of the Supreme or District Courts shall be nominated or elected to any other than a judicial office in this State.

Sec. 20. [Style of process] All writs and processes shall issue, and all prosecution shall be conducted in the name of "The State of New Mexico."

Sec. 21. [Conservators of the peace] Justices of the Supreme Court in the State, district judges in their respective districts, and justices of the peace in their respective counties, shall be conservators of the peace. District judges and justices of the peace may hold preliminary examinations in criminal cases.

Sec. 22. [County clerk] Until otherwise provided by law, a county clerk shall be elected in each county who shall, in the county for which he is elected, perform all the duties now performed by the clerks of the District Courts and clerks of the Probate Courts.

Sec. 23. [Probate courts] A Probate Court is hereby established for each county, which shall be a Court of Record, and, until otherwise provided by law shall have the same jurisdiction as is now exercised by the Probate Courts of the Territory of New Mexico. The Legislature shall have power from time to time to confer upon the Probate Court in any county in this State, general civil jurisdiction co-extensive with the county; provided, however, that such court shall not have jurisdiction in civil cases in which the matter in controversy shall exceed in value one thousand dollars, exclusive of interest; nor in any action for malicious prosecution, divorce and alimony, slander and libel; nor in any action against officers for misconduct in office; nor in any action for the specific performance of contracts for the sale of real estate; nor in any action for the possession of land; nor in any matter wherein the title or boundaries of land may be in dispute or drawn in question; nor to grant writs of injunction, habeas corpus or extraordinary writs. Jurisdiction may be conferred upon the judges of said court to act as examining and committing magistrates in criminal cases, and upon said courts for the trial of misdemeanors in which the punishment cannot be imprisonment in the penitentiary, or in which the fine cannot be in excess of one thousand dollars. A jury for the trial of such cases shall consist of six men.

Any civil or criminal case pending in the Probate Court, in which the probate judge is disqualified, shall be transferred to the District Court of the same county for trial.

Sec. 24. [District attorneys] There shall be a district attorney for each judicial district, who shall be learned in the law, and who shall have been a resident of New Mexico for three years next prior to his election, shall be the law officer of the State and of the counties within his district, shall be elected for a term of four years, and shall perform such duties and receive such salary as may be prescribed by law.

The Legislature shall have the power to provide for the election of additional district attorneys in any judicial district and the district attorneys shall serve; but no district attorney shall be elected for any district of which he is not a resident.

Sec. 25. [Judicial districts] The State shall be divided into eight judicial districts, as follows:

First district. The counties of Santa Fe, Rio Arriba and San Juan.

Second district. The counties of Bernalillo, McKinley and Sandoval.

Third district. The counties of Dona Ana, Otero, Lincoln and Torrance.

Fourth district. The counties of San Miguel, Mora and Guadalupe.

Fifth district. The counties of Eddy, Chaves, Roosevelt and Curry.

Sixth district. The counties of Grant and Luna.

Seventh district. The counties of Socorro, Valencia and Sierra.

Eighth district. The counties of Taos, Colfax, Union and Quay.

In case of the creation of new counties the Legislature shall have power to attach them to any contiguous district for judicial purposes.

Sec. 26. [Justices of peace] Justices of the peace, police magistrates and constables shall be elected in and for such precincts or districts as are or may be provided by law. Such justices and police magistrates shall not have jurisdiction in any matter in which the title to real estate or the boundaries of land may be in dispute or drawn in question, or in which the debt or sum claimed shall be in excess of two hundred dollars exclusive of interest.

Sec. 27. [Appeals] Appeals shall be allowed in all cases from the final judgments and decisions of the Probate Courts and Justices of the peace to the district courts, and in all such appeals trial shall be had de novo unless otherwise provided by law.

ARTICLE VII
ELECTIVE FRANCHISE

Section 1. [Qualifications of voters] Every male citizen of the United States who is over the age of twenty-one years, and has resided in New Mexico twelve months, in the county ninety days, and in the precinct in which he offers to vote thirty days, next preceding the election, except idiots, insane persons, persons convicted of a felonious or infamous crime, unless restored to political rights, and Indians not taxed, shall be qualified to vote at all elections for public officers. All school elections shall be held at different times from other elections. Women possessing the qualifications prescribed in this section for male electors, shall be qualified electors at all such school elections; provided, that if a majority of the qualified voters of any school district shall, not less than thirty days before any school election, present a petition to the board of county commissioners against woman suffrage in such district, the provisions of this section relating to woman suffrage shall be suspended therein, and such provision shall become again operative only upon the filing with said board of a petition signed by a majority of the qualified voters favoring the restoration of such suffrage to the proper school district.

[*Registration—corrupt practices*] The Legislature shall have the power to require the registration of the qualified electors as a requisite for voting, and shall regulate the manner, time and place of voting. The Legislature shall enact such laws as will secure the secrecy of the ballot, the purity of elections and guard against the abuses of elective franchise. Not more than two members of the board of registration and not more than two judges of election shall belong to the same political party at the time of their appointment.

Sec. 2. [Qualifications for holding office] Every citizen of the United States who is a legal resident of the State and is a qualified elector therein, shall be qualified to hold any public office in the State except as otherwise provided in this Constitution. The right to hold public office in the State of New Mexico shall not be denied or abridged on account of sex, and wherever the masculine gender is used in this Constitution, in defining the qualifications for specific officers, it shall be construed to include the feminine gender. Provided, however, that the payment of public road poll tax, school poll tax or service on juries shall not be made a prerequisite of the right of a female to vote and hold office.[7]

Sec. 3. [Racial equality] The right of any citizen of the State to vote, hold office, or sit upon juries, shall never be restricted, abridged or impaired on account of religion, race, language or color, or inability to speak, read or write the English or Spanish languages, except as may be otherwise provided in this Constitution; and the provisions of this section and of section one of this article shall never be amended

---

[7] As amended November 7, 1922. New Mexico Laws, 1921, p. 468.

except upon a vote of the people of this State in an election in which at least three-fourths of the electors voting in the whole State, and at least two-thirds of those voting in each county of the State shall vote for such amendment.

Sec. 4. [Residence] No person shall be deemed to have acquired or lost residence by reason of his presence or absence while employed in the service of the United States or of the State, nor while a student at any school.

Sec. 5. [Plurality elections] All elections shall be by ballot, and the person who receives the highest number of votes for any office shall be declared elected thereto.

Sec. 6. [Absent voting] Citizens of the State, absent from their places of legal residence, in the military or naval service of the United States or of this State, and being otherwise qualified electors, may be allowed to vote at any election for all State officers, presidential electors, Representatives in Congress, and United States Senators, and upon constitutional amendments, under such regulations and limitations as may be prescribed by law.[8]

ARTICLE VIII
TAXATION AND REVENUE [9]

Section 1. [Ad valorem taxes] Taxes levied upon tangible property shall be in proportion to the value thereof, and taxes shall be equal and uniform upon subjects of taxation of the same class.[10]

---

[8] Added by an amendment adopted November 2, 1920. New Mexico Laws, 1919, p. 370.
[9] Article VIII was revised November 3, 1914, when Joint Resolution No. 10, of the New Mexico Legislature, 1913, was approved. This revision omitted several sections, revised the wording of sections 1 and 2, and renumbered the other sections. The omitted sections were:
  Sec. 3. Legislative power to tax other subjects.
  Sec. 4. Tax limitation.
  Sec. 5. State board of equalization.
  Sec. 6. Remission of local taxes.
  Sec. 7. Renumbered as section 3.
  Sec. 8. Relinquishment of power to tax corporations.
  Sec. 9. Taxation of utility properties.
  Sec. 10. Renumbered as section 4.
  Sec. 11. Renumbered as section 5.
  Sec. 12. Renumbered as section 6.
[10] As amended November 3, 1914. New Mexico Laws, 1913, Joint Resolution No. 10.

Sec. 2. [Tax limits] Taxes levied upon real or personal property for State revenue shall not exceed four mills annually on each dollar of the assessed valuation thereof except for the support of the educational, penal and charitable institutions of the State, payment of the State debt and interest thereon; and the total annual tax levy upon such property for all State purposes exclusive of necessary levies for the State debt shall not exceed ten mills; Provided, however, that taxes levied upon real or personal tangible property for all purposes, except special levies on specific classes of property and except necessary levies for public debt, shall not exceed twenty mills annually on each dollar of the assessed valuation thereof, but laws may be passed authorizing additional taxes to be levied outside of such limitation when approved by at least a majority of the electors of the taxing district voting on such proposition.[11]

Sec. 3. [Tax exempt property] The property of the United States, the State and all the counties, towns, cities and school districts, and other municipal corporations, public libraries, community ditches and all laterals thereof, all church property, all property used for educational or charitable purposes, all cemeteries not used or held for private or corporate profit, and all bonds of the State of New Mexico, and of the counties, municipalities and districts thereof, shall be exempt from taxation.

Sec. 4. [Use of public money for private profit] Any public officer making any profit out of public monies or using the same for any purpose not authorized by law, shall be deemed guilty of a felony and shall be punished as provided by law, and shall be disqualified to hold public office. All public monies not invested in interest-bearing securities shall be deposited in national banks in this State or in banks or trust companies incorporated under the laws of the State, and the interest derived therefrom shall be applied in the manner prescribed by law.

Sec. 5. [Homestead and veterans exemption] The Legislature may exempt from taxation property of each head of a family to the amount of two hundred dollars, and the property of every

---

[11] As amended September 19, 1933. New Mexico Laws, 1933, p. 541.

honorably discharged soldier, sailor, marine and army nurse, and the widow of every soldier, sailor or marine, who served in the armed forces of the United States at any time during the period in which the United States was regularly and officially engaged in any war, in the sum of two thousand dollars. Provided, that in every case where exemption is claimed on the ground of the claimant having served with the military or naval forces of the United States as aforesaid, the burden of proving actual and bona fide ownership of such property, upon which exemption is claimed, shall be upon the claimant.[12]

Sec. 6. [Assessment of land] Lands held in large tracts shall not be assessed for taxation at any lower value per acre [than [13]] lands of the same character or quality and similarly situated, held in smaller tracts. The plowing of land shall not be considered as adding value thereto for the purpose of taxation.

Sec. 7. [Judgments against local officers] No execution shall issue upon any judgment rendered against the board of county commissioners of any county, or against any incorporated city, town or village, school district or board of education, upon any judgment recovered against him in his official capacity, and for which the county, incorporated city, town or village, school district or board of education is liable, but the same shall be paid out of the proceeds of a tax levy as other liabilities of counties, incorporated cities, towns or villages, school districts or boards of education, and when so collected shall be paid by the county treasurer to the judgment creditor.[14]

ARTICLE IX
STATE, COUNTY AND MUNICIPAL INDEBTEDNESS

Section 1. [Territorial debts] The State hereby assumes the debts and liabilities of the Territory of New Mexico, and the debts of the counties thereof which were valid and subsist-

[12] As amended November 7, 1922. New Mexico Laws, 1921, p. 470.
[13] The enrolled copy reads "then."
[14] Added by the revision of Article VIII, November 3, 1914. New Mexico Laws, 1913, Joint Resolution No. 10.

ing on June twentieth, nineteen hundred and ten, and pledges its faith and credit for the payment thereof. The Legislature shall, at its first session, provide for the payment or refunding thereof by the issue and sale of bonds or otherwise.

Sec. 2. [County debts] No county shall be required to pay any portion of the debt of any other county so assumed by the State, and the bonds of Grant and Santa Fe counties which were validated, approved and confirmed by act of Congress of January sixteenth, eighteen hundred and ninety-seven, shall be paid as hereinafter provided.

Sec. 3. [State bonds] The bonds authorized by law to provide for the payment of such indebtedness shall be issued in three series, as follows:

Series A. To provide for the payment of such debts and liabilities of the Territory of New Mexico.

Series B. To provide for the payment of such debts of said counties.

Series C. To provide for the payment of the bonds and accrued interest thereon of Grant and Santa Fe counties which were validated, approved and confirmed by act of Congress, January sixteenth, eighteen hundred and ninety-seven.

Sec. 4. [Sale of lands for bond payments] The proper officers of the State shall, as soon as practicable, select and locate the one million acres of land granted to the State by Congress for the payment of the said bonds of Grant and Santa Fe counties, and sell the same or sufficient thereof to pay the interest and principal of the bonds of Series C issued as provided in section three thereof. The proceeds of rentals and sales of said land shall be kept in a separate fund and applied to the payment of the interest and principal of the bonds of Series C. Whenever there is not sufficient money in said fund to meet the interest and sinking fund requirements therefor, the deficiency shall be paid out of any funds of the State not otherwise appropriated, and shall be repaid to the State or to the several counties which may have furnished any portion thereof under a general levy, out of the proceeds subsequently received of rentals and sales of said lands.

Any money received by the State from rentals and sales of said lands in excess of the amounts required for the purposes above mentioned shall be paid into the current and permanent school funds of the state respectively.

Sec. 5. [Remission of county debts to state] The Legislature shall never enact any law releasing any county, or any of the taxable property therein, from its obligation to pay to the State any moneys expended by the State by reason of its assumption or payment of the debt of such county.

Sec. 6. [Militia warrants] No law shall ever be passed by the Legislature validating or legalizing, directly or indirectly, the militia warrants alleged to be outstanding against the Territory of New Mexico, or any portion thereof; and no such warrant shall be prima facie or conclusive evidence of the validity of the debt purporting to be evidenced thereby or by any other militia warrant. This provision shall not be construed as authorizing any suit against the State.

Sec. 7. [Debt limit] The State may borrow money not exceeding the sum of two hundred thousand dollars in the aggregate to meet casual deficits or failure in revenue, or for necessary expenses. The State may also contract debts to suppress insurrection and to provide for the public defense.

Sec. 8. [Bonding procedure]. No debt other than those specified in the preceding section shall be contracted by or on behalf of this State, unless authorized by law for some specified work or object; which law shall provide for an annual tax levy sufficient to pay the interest and to provide a sinking fund to pay the principal of such debt within fifty years from the time of the contracting thereof. No such law shall take effect until it shall have been submitted to the qualified electors of the State and have received a majority of all the votes cast thereon at a general election, such law shall be published in at least one newspaper in each county of the State, if one be published therein, once each week, for four successive weeks next preceding such election. No debt shall be so created if the total indebtedness of the State, exclusive of the debts of the territory, and the several counties thereof, assumed by the State, would thereby be made to exceed one per centum of the assessed valuation of all the property subject to taxation in the state as shown by the preceding general assessment.

Sec. 9. [Use of debt proceeds] Any money borrowed by the State, or any county, district or municipality thereof, shall be applied to the purpose for which it was obtained, or to repay such loan, and to no other purpose whatever.

Sec. 10. [Purposes of county debts] No county shall borrow money except for the purpose of erecting necessary public buildings or construction or repairing public roads and bridges, and in such cases only after the proposition to create such debt shall have been submitted to the qualified electors of the county who paid a property tax therein during the preceding year and approved by a majority of those voting thereon. No bonds issued for such purpose shall run for more than fifty years.

Sec. 11. [School district debts] No school district shall borrow money, except for the purpose of erecting and furnishing school buildings or purchasing school grounds, and in such cases only when the proposition to create the debt shall have been submitted to a vote of such qualified electors of the district as are owners of real estate within such school district, and a majority of those voting on the question shall have voted in favor of creating such debt. No school district shall ever become indebted in an amount exceeding six per centum on the assessed valuation of the taxable property within such school district, as shown by the preceding general assessment.[15]

Sec. 12. [Municipal debts] No city, town or village shall contract any debt except by an ordinance which shall be irreparable until the indebtedness therein provided for shall have been fully paid or discharged, and which shall specify the purposes to which the funds to be raised shall be applied and which shall provide for the levy of a tax, not exceeding twelve mills on the dollar upon all taxable property within such city, town or village, sufficient to pay the interest on, and to extinguish the principal of, such debt within fifty years. The proceeds of such tax shall be

[15] As amended September 19, 1933. New Mexico Laws, 1933, p. 538.

applied only to the payment of such interest and principal. No such debt shall be created unless the question of incurring the same shall, at a regular election for councilmen, aldermen or other officers of such city, town or village, have been submitted to a vote of such qualified electors thereof as have paid a property tax therein during the preceding year, and a majority of those voting on the question, by ballot deposited in a separate ballot box, shall have voted in favor of creating such a debt.

Sec. 13. [Local debt limits] No county, city, town or village shall ever become indebted to an amount in the aggregate, including existing indebtedness, exceeding four per centum on the value of the taxable property within such county, city, town or village, as shown by the last preceding assessment for State or county taxes; and all bonds or obligations issued in excess of such amount shall be void, provided, that any city, town or village may contract debts in excess of such limitation for the construction or purchase of a system of supplying water, or of a sewer system, for such city, town or village.

Sec. 14. [Loan of public credit] Neither the State, nor any county, school district, or municipality, except as otherwise provided in this Constitution, shall directly or indirectly lend or pledge its credit, or make any donation to or in aid of any person, association or public or private corporation, or in aid of any private enterprise for the construction of any railroad; provided nothing herein shall be construed to prohibit the State or any county or municipality from making provision for the care and maintenance of sick and indigent persons.

Sec. 15. [Refunding bonds] Nothing in this article shall be construed to prohibit the issue of bonds for the purpose of paying or refunding any valid State, county, district or municipal bonds and it shall not be necessary to submit the question of the issue of such bonds to a vote as herein provided.

Sec. 16. [State highway bonds] Laws enacted by the fifth Legislature authorizing the issue or sale of State highway bonds for the purpose of providing funds for the construction and improvement of State highways and to enable the State to meet and secure allotments of federal funds to aid in construction and improvements of roads, and laws so enacted authorizing the issue and sale of State highway debentures to anticipate the collection of revenues from motor vehicle licenses and other revenues provided by law for the State Road Fund, shall take effect without submitting them to the electors of the State, and notwithstanding that the total indebtedness of the State may thereby temporarily exceed one per centum of the assessed valuation of all property subject to taxation in the State. Provided, that the total amount of such State highway bonds payable from proceeds of taxes levied on property outstanding at any time shall not exceed two million dollars. The Legislature shall not enact any law which will decrease the amount of the annual revenues pledged for the payment of State highway debentures or which will divert any of such revenues to any other purpose so long as any of the said debentures issued to anticipate the collection thereof remain unpaid.[16]

ARTICLE X
COUNTY AND MUNICIPAL CORPORATIONS

Section 1. [Organization of counties] The Legislature shall at its first session classify the counties and fix salaries for all county officers, which shall also apply to those elected at the first election under this Constitution. And no county officer shall receive to his own use any fees or emoluments other than the annual salary provided by law, and all fees earned by any officer shall be by him collected and paid into the treasury of the county.

Sec. 2. [Terms of county officers] All county officers shall be elected for a term of two years, and after having served two consecutive terms, shall be ineligible to hold any county office for two consecutive years thereafter.[17]

Sec. 3. [Removal of county seats] No county seat, where there are county build-

---

[16] Added by an amendment adopted November 7, 1922. New Mexico Laws, 1921, p. 473.

[17] As amended November 3, 1914. New Mexico Laws, 1913, p. 170.

ings, shall be removed unless three-fifths of the votes cast by qualified electors on the question of removal at an election called and held as now or hereafter provided by law, be in favor of such removal. The proposition of removal shall not be submitted in the same county oftener than once in eight years.

ARTICLE XI
CORPORATIONS OTHER THAN MUNICIPAL

Section 1. [State corporation commission] A permanent commission to consist of three members is hereby created, which shall be known as the "State Corporation Commission."

Sec. 2. [Membership of corporation commission] The members of the commission shall be elected for the term of six years; provided that those chosen at the first election for State officers shall immediately qualify and classify themselves by lot, so that one of them shall hold office until two years, one until four years, and one until six years from and after January first, nineteen hundred and thirteen; and thereafter one commissioner shall be elected at each general election.

Sec. 3. [Disqualifications for corporation commissioners] No officer, agent or employee of any railway, express, telegraph, telephone, sleeping car, or other transportation or transmission company, while representing such company, nor any person financially interested therein, shall hold office as a member of the commission, or perform any of the duties thereof, and no commissioner shall be qualified to act upon any matter pending before the commission, in which he is interested, either as principal, agent or attorney.

Sec. 4. [Staff and procedure of commission] The commission shall annually elect one of its members chairman and shall have one clerk, and such other officers, assistants and subordinates as may be prescribed by law, all of whom shall be appointed and subject to removal by the commission. The commission shall prescribe its own rules of order and procedure, except so far as specified in this Constitution. The Attorney-General of the State, or his legally authorized representative, shall be the attorney for the commission.

Sec. 5. [Expenses of commission] The Legislature shall provide suitable quarters for the commission, and funds for its lawful expenses, including necessary traveling expenses, witness fees and mileage and costs of executing process issued by the commission or the Supreme Court or the District Courts. The salary of each commissioner shall be three thousand dollars per annum, payable quarterly.

Sec. 6. [Duties of corporation commission] Subject to the provisions of this Constitution, and of such requirements, rules and regulations as may be prescribed by law, the State Corporation Commission shall be the department of government through which shall be issued all charters for domestic corporations and amendments or extensions thereof, and all licenses to foreign corporations to do business in this State; and through which shall be carried out all of the provisions of this Constitution relating to corporations and the laws made in pursuance thereof. The commission shall prescribe the form of all reports which may be required of corporations by this Constitution or by law, and shall collect, receive and preserve such reports, and annually tabulate and publish them. All fees required by law to be paid for the filing of articles of incorporation, reports and other documents, shall be collected by the commission and paid into the State Treasury. All charters, papers and documents relating to corporations on file in the office of the Secretary of the Territory, the Commissioner of Insurance and all other territorial offices shall be transferred to the office of the commission.

Sec. 7. [Powers over carriers] The commission shall have power and be charged with the duty of fixing, determining, supervising, regulating and controlling all charges and rates of railway, express, telegraph, telephone, sleeping car, and other transportation and transmission companies and common carriers within the State; to require railway companies to provide and maintain adequate depots, stockpens, station buildings, agents and facilities for the accommodation of passengers and for receiving and delivering freight and express; and to provide and maintain necessary crossings, culverts and sidings upon and alongside of their roadbeds, whenever in the judgment of the commission the public interests demands, and, as may be reasonable and just. The commission shall also have power and be charged with the duty to make and enforce reasonable and just rules requiring the supplying of cars and equipment for the use of shippers and passengers, and to require all interstate railways, transportation companies or common carriers, to provide such reasonable safety appliances in connection with all equipment, as may be necessary and proper for the safety of its employes and the public, and as are now or may be required by the federal laws, rules and regulations governing interstate commerce. The commission shall have the power to change or alter such rates, to change alter or amend its orders, rules, regulations or determinations, and to enforce the same in the manner prescribed herein; provided, that in the matter of fixing rates of telephone and telegraph companies, due consideration shall be given to the earnings, investment and expenditure as a whole within the State. The commission shall have power to subpoena witnesses and enforce their attendance before the commission, through any District Court or the Supreme Court of the State, and through such court to punish for contempt; and it shall have power, upon a hearing to determine and decide any question given to it herein, and in case of failure or refusal of any person, company or corporation to comply with any order within the time limit therein unless an order of removal shall have been taken from such order by the company or corporation to the Supreme Court of this State, it shall immediately become the duty of the commission to remove such order, with the evidence adduced upon the hearing, with the documents in the case, to the Supreme Court of this State. Any company, corporation or common carrier which does not comply with the order of the commission within the time limited therefor, may file with the commission a petition to remove such cause to the Supreme Court, and in the event of such removal by the company, corporation or common carrier, or other party to such hearing, the Supreme Court may, upon application in its discretion, or of its own motion, require or authorize additional evidence to be taken in such cause; but in the event of removal by the commission, upon failure of the company, corporation or common carrier, no additional evidence shall be allowed. The Supreme Court, for the consideration of such causes arising hereunder, shall be in session at all times and shall give precedence in such causes.

[*Appeals to supreme court*] Any party to such hearing before the commission shall have the same right to remove the order entered therein to the Supreme Court of the State, as given under the provisions hereof to the company or corporation against which such order is directed.

In addition to the other powers vested in the Supreme Court by this Constitution and the laws of the State, the said court shall have the power and it shall be its duty to decide such cases on their merits, and carry into effect its judgments, orders and decrees, made in such cases, by fine, forfeiture, mandamus, injunction and contempt or other appropriate proceedings.

Sec. 8. [**Hearings**] The commission shall determine no question nor issue any order in relation to the matter specified in the preceding section, until after a public hearing held upon ten days' notice to the parties concerned, except in case of default after such notice.

Sec. 9. [**Regulation of rates**] It is hereby made the duty of the commissioners to exercise constant diligence in informing themselves of the rates and charges of transportation and transmission companies and common carriers engaged in the transportation of passengers and property from points in this State to points beyond its limits, and from points in other states to points in this State, and, whenever it shall come to the knowledge of the commission by complaint or in any other manner, that the rate charged by any transportation or transmission company or common carriers on interstate business is unjust, excessive or unreasonable, or that such rates discriminate against the citizens of the State, and in the judgment of the commission such complaint is well founded and the public welfare involved, the commission shall institute and prosecute to a final determination before the Interstate Commerce Commission or Commerce Court, or any lawful authority having jurisdiction in the premises, such proceedings as it may deem expedient to obtain such relief as conditions may require.

Sec. 10. [Long and short hauls] No transportation or transmission company or common carrier shall charge or receive any greater compensation, in the aggregate, for the transportation as interstate commerce, of passengers, or a like kind of property, or for the transmission of the same kind of message, between points in this State, for a shorter than a longer distance over the same line or route in the same direction, the shorter being included within the longer distance; but this section shall not be construed as authorizing any such company or common carrier to charge or receive as great compensation for a shorter as for a longer distance; provided, that telegraph and telephone companies, may in certain cases, with the approval of the commission, base their charges upon the airline distances instead of the distances actually traveled by the messages. The commission may from time to time authorize any such company or common carrier to disregard the foregoing provisions of this section, by charging such rates as the commission may prescribe as "just and equitable between such company or common carrier and the public, to or from any junction or competitive points, or localities, or where the competition of points located without or within this State may necessitate the prescribing of special rates for the protection of the commerce of this State, or in cases of general epidemic, pestilence, calamitous visitations and other exigencies. This section shall not apply to mileage tickets or to any special excursion or commutation rates; nor to special rates for services rendered in the interest of any public or charitable object, when such tickets or rates shall have been prescribed or authorized by the commission, nor shall it apply to special rates for services rendered to the United States or this State.

Sec. 11. [Inspection of corporate books — reports] The commission shall have the right at all times to inspect the books, papers and records of all such companies and common carriers doing business in this State, and to require from such companies and common carriers from time to time special reports and statements, under oath concerning their business. The commissioners shall have the power to administer oaths and to certify to their official acts.

Sec. 12. [Acceptance of constitution by corporations] No corporation in existence at the time of the adoption of this Constitution shall have the benefit of any future legislation, nor shall any amendment or extension to its charters be granted, until such corporation shall have filed in the office of the commission an acceptance of the provisions of this Constitution; provided, however, that whether or not they file such acceptance, such corporations shall be subject to the provisions of this Constitution and the laws of this State.

GENERAL PROVISIONS

Sec. 13. [General corporation laws] The Legislature shall provide for the organization of corporations by general law. All laws relating to corporations may be altered, amended or repealed by the Legislature, at any time, when necessary for the public good and general welfare, and all corporations doing business in this State, may, as to such business be regulated, limited or restrained by laws not in conflict with the Constitution of the United States or of this Constitution.

Sec. 14. [Police power] The police power of this State is supreme over all corporations as well as individuals.

Sec. 15. [Discriminations by railroads] Every railroad, car or express company shall respectively receive and transport, without delay or discrimination, each other's cars, tonnage and passengers, under such rules and regulations as may be prescribed by the commission.

Sec. 16. [Discriminations by telephone and telegraph lines] All telephone and telegraph lines, operated for hire, shall receive and transmit each other's messages without delay or discrimination, and make and maintain connections with each other's lines, under such rules and regulations as may be prescribed by the commission.

Sec. 17. [Right of railroad to cross or connect with other road] Any railroad, corporation or association organized for the purpose, shall have the right to construct and operate a railroad between any point within this State or elsewhere, and to connect at the State line or elsewhere with railroads of other states; and, under such terms, order or permission as may be granted in each instance by the commission, shall have the right to cause its road to intersect, connect with or cross any other railroad.

Sec. 18. [Eminent domain] The right of eminent domain shall never be so abridged or construed as to prevent the Legislature from taking the property and franchises of incorporated companies and subjecting them to the public use, the same as the property of individuals.

ARTICLE XII
EDUCATION

Section 1. [Free public schools] A uniform system of free public schools sufficient for the education of, and open to, all the children of school age in the State shall be established and maintained.

Sec. 2. [Permanent school fund] The permanent school fund of the State shall consist of the proceeds of sales of sections two, sixteen, thirty-two and thirty-six in each township of the State, or the lands selected in lieu thereof; the proceeds of sales of all lands that have been or may hereafter be granted to the State not otherwise appropriated by the terms and conditions of the grant; such portion of the proceeds of sales of lands of the United States within the State as has been or may be granted by Congress; also all other grants, gifts and devises made to the State the purpose of which is not otherwise specified.

Sec. 3. [Aid to sectarian schools] The schools, colleges, universities and other educational institutions provided for by this Constitution shall forever remain under the exclusive control of the State, and no part of the proceeds arising from the sale or disposal of lands granted to the State by Congress, or any other funds appropriated, levied or collected for educational purposes, shall be used for the support of any sectarian, denominational or private school, or college or university.

Sec. 4. [Current school fund—taxes] All fines and forfeitures collected under general laws; the net proceeds of property that may come to the State by escheat; the rentals of all school lands and other lands granted to the State, the disposition of which is not otherwise provided for by the terms of the grant or by act of Congress; and the income derived from the permanent school fund, shall constitute the current school fund of the State. The Legislature shall provide for the levy and collection of an annual tax upon all the taxable property in the State for the maintenance of the public schools, the proceeds of such tax levy to be added to the current school fund above provided for. The current school fund shall be distributed among the school districts of the State in the proportion that the number of children of school age in each district bears to the total number of such children in the State, and shall provide for the levy and collection of additional local taxes for school purposes. A public school shall be maintained for at least five months in each year in every school district in the State.

Before making the distribution above provided for, there shall be taken from the current school fund as above created, a sufficient reserve to be distributed among school districts in which the proceeds of the annual local tax, when levied to the limit allowed by law, plus the regular quota of current school funds allotted to said districts, shall not be sufficient for the maintaining of a school for the full period of five months, and this reserve fund shall be so distributed among such districts as to enable each district to hold school for the said period.

Sec. 5. [Compulsory school attendance] Every child of school age and of sufficient physical and mental ability shall be required to attend a public or other school during such period and for such time as may be prescribed by law.

Sec. 6. [Board of education] A State Board of Education is hereby created, to consist of seven members. It shall have the control, management and direction of all public schools, under such regulations as may be provided by law. The Governor and the State Superintendent of Public Instruction shall be ex-officio members of said board and the remaining five members shall be appointed by the Governor, by and with the consent of the Senate; and shall include the head of some State educational institution, a county superintendent of schools, and one other person actually connected with educational work. The Legislature may provide for district or other school officers, subordinate to said board.

Sec. 7. [**Investment of school funds**] The principal of the permanent school fund shall be invested in the bonds of the State or Territory of New Mexico, or of any county, city, town, board of education or school district therein. The Legislature may by three-fourths vote of the members elected to each House provide that said funds may be invested in other interest-bearing securities. All bonds or other securities in which any portion of the school fund shall be invested must be first approved by the Governor, Attorney-General and Secretary of State. All losses from such funds, however occurring, shall be reimbursed by the State.

Sec. 8. [**Training of teachers**] The Legislature shall provide for the training of teachers in the normal schools or otherwise so that they may become proficient in both the English and Spanish languages, to qualify them to teach Spanish-speaking pupils and students in the public schools and educational institutions of the State; and shall provide proper means and methods to facilitate the teaching of the English language and other branches of learning to such pupils and students.

Sec. 9. [**Religious tests in schools**] No religious test shall ever be required as a condition of admission into the public schools or any educational institution of this State either as a teacher or student, and no teacher or students of such school or institution shall ever be required to attend or participate in any religious service whatsoever.

Sec. 10. [**Equality of Spanish children**] Children of Spanish descent in the State of New Mexico shall never be denied the right and privilege of admission and attendance in the public schools or other public educational institutions of the State, and they shall never be classed in separate schools, but shall forever enjoy perfect equality with other children in all public schools and educational institutions of the State, and the Legislature shall provide penalties for the violation of this section. This section shall never be amended except upon a vote of the people of this State, in an election in which at least three-fourths of the electors voting in the whole state and at least two-thirds of those voting in each county in the State shall vote for such amendment.

Sec. 11. [**Educational institutions**] The University of New Mexico at Albuquerque, the New Mexico College of Agriculture and Mechanic Arts near Las Cruces, the New Mexico School of Mines at Socorro, the New Mexico Military Institute at Roswell, the New Mexico Normal University at Las Vegas, the New Mexico Normal School at Silver City, the Spanish-American School at El Rito, the New Mexico Asylum for the Deaf and Dumb at Santa Fe, and the New Mexico Institute for the Blind at Alamogordo, are hereby confirmed as state educational institutions. The appropriations made and that may hereafter be made to the State by the United States for agricultural and mechanical colleges and experiment stations in connection therewith, shall be paid to the New Mexico College of Agriculture and Mechanic Arts.

Sec. 12. [**Federal lar grants**] All lands granted under the provisions of the act of Congress, entitled, "An Act to enable the people of New Mexico to form a Constitution and State government and be admitted to the Union on an equal footing with the original states; and to enable the people of Arizona to form a Constitution and State government and be admitted into the Union and on an equal footing with the original states, for the purpose of said several institutions, are hereby accepted and confirmed to said institutions, and shall be exclusively used for the purposes for which they are granted, provided, that one hundred and seventy thousand acres of the land granted by said act for normal school purposes are hereby equally apportioned between said three normal institutions, and the remaining thirty thousand acres thereof is reserved for a normal school which shall be established by the Legislature and located in one of the counties of Union, Quay, Curry, Roosevelt, Chaves or Eddy.

Sec. 13. [**Boards of regents**] The Legislature shall provide for the control and management of each of said institutions by a board of regents for each institution, consisting of five members to be appointed by the Governor, by and with the advice and consent of the Senate, for a term of four years, and not more than three of whom shall belong to the same political party at the time of their appointment. The duties of said boards shall be prescribed by law.

ARTICLE XIII
PUBLIC LANDS

Section 1. [Minimum sale price] All lands belonging to the Territory of New Mexico, and all lands granted, transferred or confirmed to the State by Congress, and all lands hereafter acquired, are declared to be public lands of the State to be held or disposed of as may be provided by law for the purposes for which they have been or may be granted, donated, or otherwise acquired; provided, that such of school sections two, thirty-two, sixteen and thirty-six as are not contiguous to other state lands shall not be sold within the period of ten years next after the admission of New Mexico as a State for less than ten dollars per acre.

Sec. 2. [Commissioner of public lands] The commissioner of public lands shall select, locate, classify, and have the direction, control, care and disposition of all public lands, under the provisions of the acts of Congress relating thereto and such regulations as may be provided by law.

ARTICLE XIV
PUBLIC INSTITUTIONS

Section 1. [State institutions] The penitentiary at Santa Fe, the Miners' Hospital of New Mexico at Raton, the New Mexico Insane Asylum at Las Vegas, and the New Mexico Reform School at Springer, are hereby confirmed as State institutions.

Sec. 2. [Acceptance of land grants] All lands which have been or which may be granted to the State by Congress for the purpose of said several institutions are hereby accepted for said several institutions with all other grants, donations or devises for the benefit of the same, and shall be exclusively used for the purpose for which they were or may be granted, donated or devised.

Sec. 3. [Managing boards] Each of said institutions shall be under the control and management of a board whose title, duties and powers shall be as may be provided by law. Each of said boards shall be composed of five members who shall hold office for the term of four years, and shall be appointed by the Governor by and with the consent of the Senate, and not more than three of whom shall belong to the same political party at the time of their appointment.

ARTICLE XV
AGRICULTURE AND CONSERVATION

Section 1. [Department of agriculture] There shall be a Department of Agriculture which shall be under the control of the Board of Regents of the College of Agriculture and Mechanic Arts; and the Legislature shall provide lands and funds necessary for experimental farming and demonstrating by said department.

Sec. 2. [Forests] The police power of the State shall extend to such control of private forest lands as shall be necessary for the prevention and suppression of forest fires.

ARTICLE XVI
IRRIGATION AND WATER RIGHTS

Section 1. [Existing water rights] All existing rights to the use of any waters in this State for any useful or beneficial purpose are hereby recognized and confirmed.

Sec. 2. [Appropriation of water] The unappropriated water of every natural stream, perennial or torrential, within the State of New Mexico, is hereby declared to belong to the public and to be subject to appropriation for beneficial use, in accordance with the laws of the State. Priority of appropriation shall give the better right.

Sec. 3. [Beneficial use of water] Beneficial use shall be the basis, the measure and limit of the right to the use of water.

Sec. 4. [Drainage districts] The Legislature is authorized to provide by law for the organization and operation of drainage districts and systems.

ARTICLE XVII
MINES AND MINING

Section 1. [Inspector of mines] There shall be an inspector of mines, who shall be appointed by the Governor by and with the advice and consent of the Senate, for a term of four years, and whose duties and salary shall be as prescribed by law.

Sec. 2. [Mining regulations] The Legislature shall enact laws requiring the proper ventilation of mines, the construction and maintenance of escapement shafts or slopes, and the adoption and use of appliances necessary to protect the health and secure the safety of employes therein. No children under the age of fourteen years shall be employed in mines.

ARTICLE XVIII
MILITIA

Section 1. [Composition of militia] The militia of this state shall consist of all able-bodied male citizens between the ages of eighteen and forty-five, except such as are exempt by laws of the United States or this State. The organized militia shall be called the "National Guard of New Mexico," of which the Governor shall be commander-in-chief.

Sec. 2. [Organization of militia] The Legislature shall provide for the organization, discipline and equipment of the militia, which shall conform as nearly as practicable to the organization, discipline and equipment of the regular army of the United States, and shall provide for the maintenance thereof.

ARTICLE XIX
AMENDMENTS [18]

Section 1. [Legislative proposals] Any amendment or amendments to this Constitution may be proposed in either house of the Legislature at any regular session thereof; and if a majority of all members elected to each of the two houses voting separately shall vote in favor thereof, such proposed amendment or amendments shall be entered on their respective journals with the yeas and nays thereon.

[*Publication of proposals*] The Secretary of State shall cause any such amendment or amendments to be published in at least one newspaper in every county of the State, where a newspaper is published once each week, for four consecutive weeks, in English and Spanish when newspapers in both of said languages are published in such counties, the last publication to be not more

[18] Article XIX was amended at the stipulation of Congress before the Constitution became effective. The amendment was ratified by the voters November 5, 1912.

than two weeks prior to the election at which time said amendment or amendments shall be submitted to the electors of the State for their approval or rejection; and the said amendment or amendments shall be voted upon at the next regular election held in said State after the adjournment of the Legislature proposing such amendment or amendments, or at such special election to be held not less than six months after the adjournment of said Legislature, at such time as said Legislature may by law provide. If the same be ratified by a majority of the electors voting thereon such amendment or amendments shall become part of this Constitution. If two or more amendments are proposed, they shall be so submitted as to enable the electors to vote on each of them separately: Provided, that no amendment shall apply to or affect the provisions of sections one and three of article seven, on elective franchise, and sections eight and ten of article twelve, on education, unless it be proposed by a vote of three-fourths of the members elected to each house and be ratified by a vote of the people of this State in an election at which at least three-fourths of the electors voting in the whole State and at least two-thirds of those voting in each county in the State shall vote for such amendment.

Sec. 2. [Constitutional convention] Whenever, during the first twenty-five years after the adoption of this Constitution, the Legislature, by a three-fourths vote of the members elected to each house, or after the expiration of said period of twenty-five years, by a two-thirds vote of the members elected to each house, shall deem it necessary to call a convention to revise or amend this Constitution, they shall submit the question of calling such convention to the electors at the next general election, and if a majority of the electors voting on such question at said election in the State shall vote in favor of calling a convention the Legislature shall, at the next session, provide by law for calling the same. Such convention shall consist of at least as many delegates as there are members of the House of Representatives. The Constitution adopted by such convention shall have no validity until it has been submitted to and ratified by the people.

Sec. 3. [Initiative] If this Constitution be in any way so amended as to allow laws to be enacted by direct vote of the electors the laws which may be so enacted shall be only such as might be enacted by the Legislature under the provisions of this Constitution.

Sec. 4. [Amendment of article xxi] When the United States shall consent thereto, the Legislature, by a majority vote of the members in each house, may submit to the people, the question of amending any provision of article twenty-one of this Constitution on compact with the United States to the extent allowed by the act of Congress permitting the same, and if a majority of the qualified electors who vote on any such amendment shall vote in favor thereof, the said article shall be thereby amended accordingly.

Sec. 5. [Alteration of amendment provisions] The provisions of section one of this article shall not be changed, altered, or abrogated in any manner except through a general convention called to revise this Constitution as herein provided.

ARTICLE XX
MISCELLANEOUS

Section 1. [Oath] Every person elected or appointed to any office shall before entering upon his duties, take and subscribe to an oath or affirmation that he will support the Constitution of the United States and the Constitution and laws of this State, and that he will faithfully and impartially discharge the duties of his office to the best of his ability.

Sec. 2. [Tenure of office] Every officer, unless removed, shall hold his office until his successor has duly qualified.

Sec. 3. [Date terms of office begin] The term of office of every State, county or district officer, except those elected at the first election held under this Constitution, and those elected to fill vacancies, shall commence on the first day of January next after his election.

Sec. 4. [Vacancies] If a vacancy occur in the office of district attorney, judge of the Supreme Court or District Court, or county commissioner, the Governor shall fill such vacancy by appointment, and such appointee shall hold such office until the next general election. His successor shall be chosen at such election and shall hold his office until the expiration of the original term.

Sec. 5. [Interim appointments] If, while the Senate is not in session, a vacancy occur in any office the incumbent of which was appointed by the Governor by and with the advice and consent of the Senate, the Governor shall appoint some qualified person to fill the same until the next session of the Senate; and shall then appoint by and with the advice and consent of the Senate some qualified person to fill said office for the period of the unexpired term.

Sec. 6. [Date of general elections] General elections shall be held in the State on the Tuesday after the first Monday in November, in each even numbered year.

Sec. 7. [Canvass of election returns] The returns of all elections for officers who are chosen by the electors of more than one county shall be canvassed by the county canvassing board of each county as to the vote within their respective counties. Said board shall immediately certify the number of votes received by each candidate for such office within such county, to the State Canvassing Board herein established, which shall canvass and declare the result of the election.

Sec. 8. [First election] In the event that New Mexico is admitted into the Union as a State prior to the Tuesday next after the first Monday in November in the year nineteen hundred and twelve, and if no provision has been made by the State Legislature therefor, an election shall be held in the State on the said Tuesday next after the first Monday in November, nineteen hundred and twelve, for the election of presidential electors, and such election shall be held as herein provided for the election upon the ratification of this Constitution, and the returns thereof made to, and canvassed and certified by the State Canvassing Board as herein provided in case of the election of State officers.

Sec. 9. [Fees] No officer of the State who receives a salary shall accept, or receive to his own use any compensation, fees, allowance, or emoluments for or on account of his office, in any form whatever, except the salary provided by law.

FIRST STATE CONSTITUTION

Sec. 10. [Child labor] The Legislature shall enact suitable laws for the regulation of the employment of children.

Sec. 11. [Women notaries] Women may hold the office of notary public and such other appointive offices as may be provided by law.

Sec. 12. [Official languages] For the first twenty years after this Constitution goes into effect all laws passed by the Legislature shall be published in both English and Spanish languages and thereafter such publication shall be made as the Legislature may provide.

Sec. 13. [Sacramental wines] The use of wines solely for sacramental purposes under church authority at any place within the State shall never be prohibited.

Sec. 14. [Passes] It shall not be lawful for the Governor, nor member of the State Board of Equalization, any member of the Corporation Commission, any judge of the Supreme Court or District Court, any district attorney, any county commissioner or any county assessor, during his term of office to accept, hold or use any free pass; or purchase, receive or accept transportation over any railroad within this State for himself or his family upon terms not open to the general public; and any person violating the provisions hereof, shall, upon conviction in a court of competent jurisdiction, be punished as provided in sections thirty-seven and forty of the article on legislative departments in this Constitution.

Sec. 15. [Conduct of penitentiary] The penitentiary is a reformatory and an industrial school, and all persons confined therein shall, so far as consistent with discipline and the public interest, be employed in some beneficial industry; and where a convict has a dependent family his net earnings shall be paid to said family if necessary for their support.

Sec. 16. [Liability for personal injuries] Every person, receiver or corporation owning or operating a railroad within this State shall be liable in damages for injury to, or the death of, any person in its employ, resulting from the negligence, in whole or in part, of said owner or operator, or of any of the officers, agents or employes thereof, or by reason of any defect or insufficiency, due to its negligence, in whole or in part, in its cars, engines, appliances, machinery, track, roadbed, works or other equipment.

An action for negligently causing the death of an employe as above provided shall be maintained by the executor or administrator for the benefit of the employe's surviving widow or husband and children; or if none, then his parents; or if none, then the next of kin dependent upon said deceased. The amount recovered may be distributed as provided by law. Any contract or agreement made in advance of such injury with any employe waiving or limiting any right to recover such damages shall be void.

This provision shall not be construed to affect the provisions of section two of article twenty-two of this Constitution, being the article upon schedule.

Sec. 17. [Uniform text-books] There shall be a uniform system of textbooks for the public schools which shall not be changed more than once in six years.

Sec. 18. [Convict labor] The leasing of convict labor by the State is hereby prohibited.

Sec. 19. [Eight-hour day on public works] Eight hours shall constitute a day's work in all cases of employment by and on behalf of the State or any county or municipality thereof.

Sec. 20. [Waiver of indictment] Any person held by a committing magistrate to await the action of the grand jury on a charge of felony or other infamous crime, may in open court with the consent of the court and the district attorney to be entered upon the record, waive indictment and plead to an information in the form of an indictment filed by the district attorney, and further proceedings shall then be had upon said information with like force and effect as though it were an indictment duly returned by the grand jury.

ARTICLE XXI
COMPACT WITH THE UNITED STATES

In compliance with the requirements of the act of Congress entitled "An act to enable the people of New Mexico to form a Constitution and State government and be admitted into the Union on an equal footing with the original states; and to enable the people of Arizona to form a Constitution and state government and be admitted into the Union on an equal footing with the original states," approved June twentieth, nineteen hundred and ten, it is hereby provided:

Section 1. [Freedom of religion—intoxicating liquors] Perfect toleration of religious sentiment shall be secured, and no inhabitant of this State shall ever be molested in person or property on account of his or her mode of religious worship. Polygamous or plural marriages, polygamous cohabitation, and the sale, barter, or giving of intoxicating liquors to Indians, the introduction of such liquors into the Indian country, which term shall also include all lands owned or occupied by the Pueblo Indians of New Mexico on the twentieth day of June, nineteen hundred and ten, or which are occupied by them at the time of the admission of New Mexico as a State, are forever prohibited.

Sec. 2. [Title to Indian lands] The people inhabitating this State do agree and declare that they forever disclaim all right and title to the unapportioned and ungranted public lands lying within the boundaries thereof, and to all lands lying within said boundaries owned or held by any Indian or Indian tribes, the right or title to which shall have been acquired through the United States, or any prior sovereignty; and that until the title of such Indian or Indian tribes shall have been extinguished, the same shall be and remain subject to the disposition and under the absolute jurisdiction and control of the Congress of the United States; that the lands and other property belonging to citizens of the United Sates residing without this State shall never be taxed at a higher rate than the lands and other property belonging to residents thereof; that no taxes shall be imposed by this State upon the lands or property therein belonging to or which may hereafter be acquired by the United States or reserved for its use; but nothing herein shall preclude this State from taxing as other lands, and property, outside of an Indian reservation, owned or held by any Indian save and except such lands as have been granted and acquired as aforesaid, or as may be granted or confirmed to any Indian or Indians under any act of Congress; but all such lands shall be exempt from taxation by this State so long and to such extent as the Congress of the United States has prescribed or may hereafter prescribe.

Sec. 3. [Territorial debts] The debts and liabilities of the Territory of New Mexico, and the debts of the counties thereof, which were valid and subsisting on the twentieth day of June nineteen hundred and ten, are hereby assumed and shall be paid by this State; and this State shall, as to all such debts and liabilities, be subrogated to all rights, including rights of indemnity and reimbursement, existing in favor of said Territory or any of the several counties thereof on said date. Nothing in this article shall be construed as validating or in any manner legalizing any territorial, county, municipal or other bonds, warrants, obligations, or evidence of indebtedness of, or claims against said Territory or any of the counties or municipalities thereof, which now are or may be at the time this State is admitted, invalid and illegal; nor shall the Legislature of this State pass any law in any manner validating or legalizing the same.

Sec. 4. [Public schools] Provision shall be made for the establishment and maintenance of a system of public schools which shall be open to all the children of the State and free from sectarian control, and said schools shall always be conducted in English.

Sec. 5. [Suffrage] This State shall never enact any law restricting or abridging the right of suffrage on account of race, color or previous conditions of servitude.[19]

Sec. 6. [Capital] The capital of this State shall, until changed by the electors at an election provided for by the Legislature of this State for that purpose, be at the city of Santa Fe, but no such election shall be called or provided for prior to the thirty-first day of December, nineteen hundred and twenty-five.

Sec. 7. [Reclamation projects] There are hereby reserved to the United States, with full acquiescence of the people of this State, all rights and powers for the carrying out of provisions by the United States of the act of

---

[19] As amended November 5, 1912. New Mexico Laws, 1912, p. 272.

Congress entitled, "An act appropriating the receipts from the sale and disposal of public lands in certain states and territories to the construction of irrigation works for the reclamation of arid lands," approved June seventeenth, nineteen hundred and two, and acts amendatory thereof or supplementary thereto, to the same extent as if this State had remained a territory.

Sec. 8. [Sale of liquor on Indian lands] Whenever hereafter any of the lands contained within Indian reservations or allotments in this State shall be allotted, sold, reserved or otherwise disposed of, they shall be subject for a period of twenty-five years after such allotment, sale, reservation or other disposal, to all the laws of the United States prohibiting the introduction of liquor into the Indian country, and the terms "Indian" and Indian country shall include the Pueblo Indians of New Mexico and the lands owned or occupied by them on the twentieth day of June, nineteen hundred and ten, or which are occupied by them at the time of the admission of New Mexico as a State.

Sec. 9. [Agreement to compact by state] This State and its people consent to all and singular the provisions of the said act of Congress, approved June twentieth, nineteen hundred and ten, concerning the lands by said act granted or confirmed to this State, the terms and the conditions upon which said grants and confirmations were made and the means and manner of enforcing such terms and conditions, all in every respect and particular as in said act provided.

Sec. 10. [Compact to be irrevocable] This ordinance is irrevocable without the consent of the United States and the people of this State, and no change or abrogation of this ordinance, in whole or in part, shall be made by any constitutional amendment without the consent of Congress.

Sec. 11. [Exchanges of lands] This State and its people consent to the provisions of the act of Congress, approved June 15, 1926, providing for such exchanges and the Governor and other State officers mentioned in said act are hereby authorized to execute the necessary instrument or instruments to effect the exchange of lands therein provided for with the government of the United States; provided that in the determination of values of the lands now owned by the State of New Mexico, the value of the lands, the timber thereon and mineral rights pertaining thereto shall control the determination of value. The Legislature may enact laws for carrying out the provisions hereof in accordance herewith.[20]

ARTICLE XXII
SCHEDULE

That no inconvenience may arise by reason of the change from a territorial to a state form of government, it is declared and ordained:

Section 1. [Date Constitution takes effect] This Constitution shall take effect and be in full force immediately upon the admission of New Mexico into the Union as a state.

Sec. 2. [Federal employers liability act] Until otherwise provided by law, the Act of Congress of the United States, entitled, "An Act relating to the liability of common carriers, by railroads to their employes in certain cases," approved April twenty-second, nineteen hundred and eight, and all acts amendatory thereof, shall be and remain in force in this State to the same extent that they have been in force in the Territory of New Mexico.

Sec. 3. [Federal mining inspection act] Until otherwise provided by law, the act of Congress, entitled, "An act for the protection of the lives of miners," approved March third, eighteen hundred and ninety-one, and all acts amendatory thereof, shall be and remain in force in this State to the same extent that they have been in force in the Territory of New Mexico; the words, "Governor of the State," are hereby substituted for the words "Governor of such organized Territory," and for the words "Secretary of the Interior" whenever the same appears in said act; and the chief mine inspector for the Territory of New Mexico, appointed by the President of the United States, is hereby authorized to perform the duties prescribed by said acts until superseded by the "inspector of mines" appointed by the Governor.

[20] Added by an amendment adopted November 8, 1932. New Mexico Laws, 1931, p. 302.

nor, as elsewhere provided by the Constitution, and he shall receive the same compensation from the State as he received from the United States.

Sec. 4. [Existing laws] All laws of the Territory of New Mexico in force at the time of its admission into the Union as a State, not inconsistent with this Constitution, shall be and remain in force as the laws of the State until they expire by their own limitation, or are altered or repealed; and all rights, actions, claims, contracts, liabilities and obligations, shall continue and remain unaffected by the change in the form of government.

Sec. 5. [Pardoning power] The pardoning power herein granted shall extend to all persons who have been convicted of offenses against the laws of the Territory of New Mexico.

Sec. 6. [Claims of territory] All property, real and personal, and all moneys, credits, claims and choses in action belonging to the Territory of New Mexico, shall become the property of this State; and all debts, taxes, fines, penalties, escheats and forfeitures which have accrued or may accrue to said Territory, shall inure to this State.

Sec. 7. [Obligations due territory] All recognizances, bonds, obligations and undertakings entered into or executed to the Territory of New Mexico or to any county, school district, municipality, officer or official board therein, shall remain valid according to the terms thereof, and may be sued upon and recovered by the proper authority under the State law.

Sec. 8. [Existing legal processes] All lawful process, writs, judgments, decrees, convictions, and sentences issued, rendered, had or pronounced, in force at the time of the admission of the State, shall continue and remain in force to the same extent as if the change of government had not occurred, and shall be enforced and executed under the laws of the State.

Sec. 9. [Continuance of courts] All courts existing, and all persons holding offices or appointments under the authority of said Territory at the time of the admission of the State, shall continue to hold and exercise their respective jurisdictions, functions, offices and appointments until superseded by the courts, officers or authorities provided for by this Constitution.

[Seals] Until otherwise provided by law, the seal of the Territory shall be used as the seal of the State, and the seals of the several courts, officers and official boards in the Territory shall be used as the seals of the corresponding courts, officers and official boards in the State; and for any new court, office or board created by this Constitution, a seal may be adopted by the judge of said court, or the incumbent of said office, or by the said board.

Sec. 10. [Court proceedings] All suits, indictments, criminal actions, bonds, process, matters and proceedings pending in any of the courts in the Territory of New Mexico at the time of the organization of the courts provided for in this Constitution shall be transferred to and proceed to determination in such courts of like or corresponding jurisdiction. And all civil causes of action and criminal offenses which shall have been commenced or indictment found, shall be subject to action, prosecution, indictment and review in the proper courts of the State, in like manner and to the same extent as if the State had been created and said courts established prior to the accrual of such cases and action and the commission of such offenses.

Sec. 11. [Custody of constitution] This Constitution shall be signed by the president and secretary of the Constitutional Convention, and such delegates as desire to sign the same, and shall be deposited in the office of the Secretary of the Territory where it may be signed at any time by any delegate.

Sec. 12. [Assumption of territorial debts] All lawful debts and obligations of the several counties of the Territory of New Mexico not assumed by the State and of the school districts, municipalities, irrigation districts and improvement districts, therein, existing at the time of its admission as a State, shall remain valid and unaffected by the change of government, until paid or refunded according to law; and all counties, municipalities and districts in said Territory shall continue with the same names, boundaries and rights until changed in accordance with the Constitution and laws of the State.

Sec. 13. [Ratification of constitution] This Constitution shall be submitted to the people of

New Mexico for ratification at an election to be held on the twenty-first day of January, nineteen hundred and eleven, at which election the qualified voters of New Mexico shall vote directly for or against the same, and the Governor of the Territory of New Mexico shall forthwith issue his proclamation ordering said election to be held on said day.

Except as the manner of making returns of said election and canvassing and certifying the result thereof, said election shall be held and conducted in the manner prescribed by the laws of New Mexico now in force.

Sec. 14. [Referendum ballots] The ballots cast at said election in favor of the ratification of this Constitution shall have printed or written thereon in both English and Spanish the words "For the Constitution," and those against the ratification of the Constitution shall have written or printed therein in both English and Spanish the words "Against the Constitution"; and shall be counted and returned accordingly.

Sec. 15. [Canvass of referendum election] The returns of said election shall be made by the election officers to the secretary of the Territory of New Mexico at Santa Fe, who with the Governor and the Chief Justice of said Territory, shall constitute a canvassing board, and they, or any two of them, shall meet at said city of Santa Fe on the third Monday after said election and shall canvass the same. Said canvassing board shall make and file with the secretary of the Territory of New Mexico, a certificate signed by at least two of them, setting forth the number of votes cast at said election for and against the Constitution, respectively.

Sec. 16. [Certification of vote] If a majority of the legal votes cast at said election as certified to by said canvassing board, shall be for the Constitution, it shall be deemed to be duly ratified by the people of New Mexico and the secretary of the Territory of New Mexico shall forthwith cause to be submitted to the President of the United States and to Congress for approval a certified copy of this Constitution, together with the statement of the votes cast thereon.

Sec. 17. [First election of officers] If Congress and the President approve this Constitution, and if the President approves the same and Congress fails to disapprove the same, during the next regular session thereof, the Governor of New Mexico shall, within thirty days after receipt of notification from the President certifying said facts, issue his proclamatoin for an election at which officers for a full State government, including a Governor, county officers, members of the State Legislature, two representatives in Congress to be elected at large from the State, and such other officers as the Constitution prescribes, shall be chosen by the people; said election to take place no earlier than sixty days nor later than ninety days after the date of said proclamation by the Governor ordering the same.

Sec. 18. [Canvass of first election] Said last mentioned election shall be held, the returns thereof made, canvassed and certified to by the secretary of said territory, in the same manner, and the same laws, including those as to qualifications of electors, shall be applicable thereto, as hereinbefore prescribed for holding, making of the returns, canvassing and certifying, the same, of the election for the ratification or rejection of the Constitution.

When said election of State and county officers, members of the Legislature, representatives in Congress, and other officers provided for in this Constitution, shall be held and the returns thereof made, canvassed and certified as hereinafter provided, the Governor of the Territory of New Mexico shall immediately ratify the result of said election as canvassed and certified as hereinbefore provided, to the President of the United States.

Sec. 19. [Date officers take office] Within thirty days after the issuance by the President of the United States of his proclamation announcing the result of said election so ascertained, all officers elected at such election, except members of the Legislature, shall take the oath of office and give bond as required by the Constitution or by the laws of the Territory of New Mexico in case of like officers in the territory, county or district, and shall thereupon enter upon the duties of their respective officers to give other additional bonds as a condition of their continuance in office.

Sec. 20. [Convening of first legislature] The Governor of the State, immediately upon his qualifying and entering upon the duties of his office, shall issue his proclamation convening the Legislature at the seat of government on a day to be specified therein, not less than thirty nor more than sixty days after the date of said proclamation.

The members-elect of the Legislature shall meet on the day specified, take the oath required by this Constitution and within ten days after organization shall proceed to the election of two senators of the United States for the State of New Mexico, in the manner prescribed by the Constitution and laws of the United States; and the Governor and Secretary of State of New Mexico shall certify the election of the senators and representatives in Congress in the manner required by law.

Sec. 21. [Supplementary legislation] The Legislature shall pass all necessary laws to carry into effect the provisions of this Constitution.

Sec. 22. [Terms of first officers] The term of office of all officers elected at the election aforesaid shall commence on the date of their qualification and shall expire at the same time as if they had been elected on the Tuesday next after the first Monday of November in the year nineteen hundred and twelve.

Done in open convention at the city of Santa Fe, in the Territory of New Mexico, this twenty-first day of November, in the year of our Lord, one thousand nine hundred and ten.

ARTICLE XXIII
[INTOXICATING LIQUORS [21]]

[21] Added by an amendment (New Mexico Laws, 1917, p. 352) and repealed by Article XXV.

ARTICLE XXIV
RESERVING MINERAL ROYALTIES [22]

Leases and other contracts, reserving a royalty to the State, for the development and production of any and all minerals on lands granted or confirmed to the State of New Mexico by the Act of Congress of June 20, 1910, entitled "An Act to enable the people of New Mexico to form a Constitution and State government and be admitted into the Union on an equal footing. with the original states," may be made under such provisions relating to the necessity or requirement for or the mode and manner of appraisement, advertisement and competitive bidding, and containing such terms and provisions, as may be provided by Act of the Legislature; the rentals, royalties and other proceeds therefrom to be applied and conserved in accordance with the provisions of said Act of Congress for the support or in aid of the common schools, or for the attainment of the respective purposes for which the several grants were made.

ARTICLE XXV
REPEAL OF ARTICLE XXIII [23]

Section 1. [Prohibition repeal] That article twenty-three (XXIII) of the Constitution of the State of New Mexico, entitled "Intoxicating Liquors" is hereby repealed.

Sec. 2. [Liquor control laws] That all laws enacted at the regular session of the Eleventh State Legislature, relating to intoxicating liquors shall be as valid as if the same were enacted after the adoption of this amendment, or after any change in the Constitution or laws of the United States relating to intoxicating liquors.

[22] Added by an amendment adopted November 6, 1928. New Mexico Laws, 1927, p. 485.
[23] Added by an amendment adopted September 19, 1933. New Mexico Laws, 1933, p. 537.

SELECTED DOCUMENTS

The documents selected for this section have been chosen to reflect the interests or attitudes of the contemporary observer or writer. Documents relating specifically to the constitutional development of New Mexico will be found in volume seven of <u>Sources and Documents of United States Constitutions</u>, a companion reference collection to the Columbia University volumes previously cited.

DE VACA'S JOURNEY TO NEW MEXICO

Source: <u>America. Great Crises In Our History Told by Its Makers</u>. Chicago: Americanization Department. Veterans of Foreign Wars of the United States. 1925.

DE VACA'S JOURNEY TO NEW MEXICO

From Cabeza de Vaca's Relation

THE SUCCESS of Cortez in Mexico led many Spanish adventurers on expeditions into various parts of the New World. And among them none was more thrilling than de Vaca's wanderings from the Gulf of Mexico through the present States of Texas and New Mexico.

De Vaca was treasurer of Navarez's expedition that sailed from Spain in 1527, and landed at the present Apalache Bay on the coast of Florida. Navarez lost his life, and most of his men were either killed by savages or died of disease and starvation. De Vaca was held six years a captive, and finally escaped with two companions and a negro slave.

After their escape they pushed on northwards and westwards, enduring incredible hardships, until they finally came upon some other Spanish explorers upon the River Petatlan, on the 1st of April, 1536. Returning to Spain, de Vaca published a "Relation" of his travels, from which this account is taken.

WE TOLD these people that we desired to go where the sun sets; and they said inhabitants in that direction were remote. We commanded them to send and make known our coming; but they strove to excuse themselves the best they could, the people being their enemies, and they did not wish to go to them. Not daring to disobey, however, they sent two women, one of their own, the other a captive from that people; for the women can negotiate even though there be war. We followed them, and stopped at a place where we agreed to wait. They tarried five days; and the Indians said they could not have found anybody.

We told them to conduct us towards the north; and they answered, as before, that except afar off there were no people in that direction, and nothing to eat, nor could water be found. Notwithstanding all this, we persisted, and said we desired to go in that course. They still tried to excuse themselves in the best manner possible. At this we became offended, and one night I went out to sleep in the woods apart from them; but directly they came to where I was, and remained all night without sleep, talking to me in great fear, telling me how terrified they were, beseeching us to be no longer angry, and said that they would lead us in the direction it was our wish to go, though they knew they should die on the way. . . .

While we were among these people, which was more than fifteen days, we saw no one speak to another, nor did we see an infant smile: the only one that cried they took off to a distance, and with the sharp teeth of a rat they scratched it from the shoulders down nearly to the end of the legs. Seeing this cruelty, and offended at it, I asked why they did so: they said for chastisement, because the child had wept in my presence. . . .

From that place onward was another usage. Those who knew of our approach did not come out to receive us on the road as the others had done, but we found them in their houses, and they had made others for our reception. They were all seated with their faces turned to the wall, their heads down, the hair brought before their eyes, and their property placed in a heap in the middle of the house. From this place they began to give us many blankets of skin; and they had nothing they did not bestow. They have the finest persons of any people we saw, of the greatest activity and strength, who best understood us and intelligently answered our inquiries. We called them the Cow nation, because most of the cattle killed are slaughtered in their neighborhood, and along up that river for over fifty leagues they destroy great numbers.

They go entirely naked after the manner of the first we saw. The women are dressed with deer skin, and some few men, mostly the aged, who are incapable of fighting. The country is very populous. We asked how it was they did not plant maize. They answered it was that they might not lose what they should put in the ground; that the rains had failed for two years in succession, and the seasons were so dry the seed had everywhere been taken by the moles, and they could not venture to plant again until after water had fallen copiously. They begged us to tell the sky to rain, and to pray for it, and we said we would do so. We also desired to know whence they got the maize, and they told us from where the sun goes down; there it grew throughout the region, and the nearest was by that path. . . .

Doubting what it would be best to do, and which way we should choose for suitableness and support, we remained two days with these Indians, who gave us beans and pumpkins for our subsistence. Their method of cooking is so new that for its strangeness I desire to speak of it; thus it may be seen and remarked how curious and diversified are the contrivances and ingenuity of the human family. Not having discovered the use of pipkins, to boil what they would eat, they fill the half of a large calabash with water, and throw on the fire many stones of such as are most convenient and readily take the heat. When hot, they are taken up with tongs of sticks and dropped into the calabash until the water in it boils from the fervor of the stones. Then whatever is to be cooked is put in, and until it is done they continue taking out cooled stones and throwing in hot ones. Thus they boil their food.

TWO days being spent while we tarried, we resolved to go in search of the maize. We did not wish to follow the path leading to where the cattle are, because it is towards the north, and for us very circuitous, since we ever held it certain that going towards the sunset we must find what we desired. . . .

As the sun went down, upon some plains that lie between chains of very great mountains, we found a people who for the third part of the year eat nothing but the powder of straw, and, that being the season when we passed, we also had to eat of it, until reaching permanent habitations, where was abundance of maize brought together. They gave us a large quantity in grain and flour, pumpkins, beans, and shawls of cotton. With all these we loaded our guides, who went back the happiest creatures on earth. We gave thanks to God, our Lord, for having brought us where we had found so much food.

Some houses are of earth, the rest all of cane mats. From this point we marched through more than a hundred leagues of country, and continually found settled domicils, with plenty of maize and beans. The people gave us many deer and cotton shawls better than those of New Spain, many beads and certain corals found on the South sea, and fine turquoises that come from the north. Indeed they gave us everything they had. To me they gave five emeralds made into arrow-heads, which they use at their singing and dancing. They appeared to be very precious. I asked whence they got these; and they said the stones were brought from some lofty mountains that stand towards the north, where were populous towns and very large houses, and that they were purchased with plumes and the feathers of parrots.

Among this people the women are treated with more decorum than in any part of the Indias we had visited. They wear a shirt of cotton that falls as low as the knee, and over it half sleeves with skirts reaching to the ground, made of dressed deer skin. It opens in front and is brought close with straps of leather. They soap this with a certain root that cleanses well, by which they are enabled to keep it becomingly. Shoes are worn. The people all came to us that we should touch and bless them, they being very urgent, which we could accomplish only with great labor, for sick and well all wished to go with a benediction. . . .

Throughout all these countries the people who were at war immediately made friends, that they might come to meet us, and bring what they possessed. In this way we left all the land at peace, and we taught all the inhabitants by signs, which they understood, that in heaven was a Man we called God, who had created the sky and the earth; him we worshiped and had for our master; that we did what he commanded and from his hand came all good; and would they do as we did, all would be well with them. So ready of apprehension we found them that, could we have had the use of language by which to make ourselves perfectly understood, we should have left them all Christians. Thus much we gave them to understand the best we could. And afterward, when the sun rose, they opened their hands together with loud shouting towards the heavens, and then drew them down all over their bodies. They did the same again when the sun went down. They are a people of good condition and substance, capable in any pursuit. . . .

WE passed through many territories and found them all vacant: their inhabitants wandered fleeing among the mountains, without daring to have houses or till the earth for fear of Christians. The sight was one of infinite pain to us, a land very fertile and beautiful, abounding in springs and streams, the hamlets deserted and burned, the people thin and weak, all fleeing or in concealment. As they did not plant, they appeased their keen hunger by eating roots and the bark of trees. We bore a share in the famine along the whole way; for poorly could these unfortunates provide for us, themselves being so reduced they looked as though they would willingly die. They brought shawls of those they had concealed because of the Christians, presenting them to us; and they related how the Christians at other times had come through the land, destroying and burning the towns, carrying away half the men, and all the women and the boys, while those who had been able to escape were wandering about fugitives. We found them so alarmed they dared not remain anywhere. They would not nor could they till the earth, but preferred to die rather than live in dread of such cruel usage as they received. Although these showed themselves greatly delighted with us, we feared that on our arrival among those who held the frontier, and fought against the Christians, they would treat us badly, and revenge upon us the conduct of their enemies; but, when God our Lord was pleased to bring us there, they began to dread and respect us as the others had done, and even somewhat more, at which we no little wondered. Thence it may at once be seen that, to bring all these people to be Christians and to the obedience of the Imperial Majesty, they must be won by kindness, which is a way certain, and no other is.

They took us to a town on the edge of a range of mountains, to which the ascent is over difficult crags. We found many people there collected out of fear of the Christians. They received us well, and presented us all they had. They gave us more than two thousand back-loads of maize, which we gave to the distressed and hungered beings who guided us to that place. The next day we despatched four messengers through the country, as we were accustomed to do, that they should call together all the rest of the Indians at a town distant three days' march. We set out the day after with all the people. The tracks of the Christians and marks where they slept were continually seen. At mid-day we met our messengers, who told us they had found no Indians, that they were roving and hiding in the forests, fleeing that the Christians might not kill nor make them slaves; the night before they had observed the Christians from behind trees, and discovered what they were about, carrying away many people in chains. . . .

WHEN we saw sure signs of Christians, and heard how near we were to them, we gave thanks to God our Lord for having chosen to bring us out of a captivity so melancholy and wretched. The delight we felt let each one conjecture, when he shall remember the length of time we were in that country, the suffering and perils we underwent. That night I entreated my companions that one of them should go back three days' journey after the Christians who were moving about over the country, where we had given assurance of protection. Neither of them received this proposal well, excusing themselves because of weariness and exhaustion; and although either might have done better than I, being more youthful and athletic, yet seeing their unwillingness, the next morning I took the negro with eleven Indians, and, following the Christians by their trail, I traveled ten leagues, passing three villages, at which they had slept.

The day after I overtook four of them on horseback, who were astonished at the sight of me, so strangely habited as I was, and in company with Indians. They stood staring at me a length of time, so confounded that they neither hailed me nor drew near to make an inquiry. I bade them take me to their chief: accordingly we went together half a league to the place where was Diego de Alcaraz, their captain.

After we had conversed, he stated to me that he was completely undone; he had not been able in a long time to take any Indians; he knew not which way to turn, and his men had well begun to experience hunger and fatigue. . . .

FIVE days having elapsed, Andrés Dorantes and Alonzo del Castillo arrived with those who had been sent after them. They brought more than six hundred persons of that community, whom the Christians had driven into the forests, and who had wandered in concealment over the land. Those who accompanied us so far had drawn them out, and given them to the Christians, who thereupon dismissed all the others they had brought with them. Upon their coming to where I was, Alcaraz begged that we would summon the people of the towns on the margin of the river, who straggled about under cover of the woods, and order them to fetch us something to eat. This last was unnecessary, the Indians being ever diligent to bring us all they could. Directly we sent our messengers to call them, when there came six hundred souls, bringing us all the maize in their possession. They fetched it in certain pots, closed with clay, which they had concealed in the earth. They brought us whatever else they had; but we, wishing only to have the provision, gave the rest to the Christians, that they might divide among themselves. After this we had many high words with them; for they wished to make slaves of the Indians we brought. . . .

The Indians, at taking their leave, told us they would do what we commanded, and would build their towns, if the Christians would suffer them; and this I say and affirm most positively, that, if they have not done so, it is the fault of the Christians. . . .

The night being passed, we set out the next day for Anhacan. The chief Alcalde besought us to tarry there, since by so doing we could be of eminent service to God and your Majesty; the deserted land was without tillage and everywhere badly wasted, the Indians were fleeing and concealing themselves in the thickets, unwilling to occupy their towns; we were to send and call them, commanding them in behalf of God and the King, to return to live in the vales and cultivate the soil.

To us this appeared difficult to effect. We had brought no native of our own, nor of those who accompanied us according to custom, intelligent in these affairs. At last we made the attempt with two captives, brought from that country, who were with the Christians we first overtook. They had seen the people who conducted us, and learned from them the great authority and command we carried and exercised throughout those parts, the wonders we had worked, the sick we had cured, and the many things besides we had done. We ordered that they, with others of the town, should go together to summon the hostile natives among the mountains and of the river Petachan, where we had found the Christians, and say to them they must come to us, that we wished to speak with them. . . .

The Indians were gone seven days, and returned with three chiefs of those revolted among the ridges, who brought with them fifteen men, and presented us beads, turquoises, and feathers. The messengers said they had not found the people of the river where we appeared, the Christians having again made them run away into the mountains. . . .

AS soon as these Indians went back, all those of that province who were friendly to the Christians, and had heard of us, came to visit us, bringing beads and feathers. We commanded them to build churches and put crosses in them: to that time none had been raised; and we made them bring their principal men to be baptized.

Then the captain made a covenant with God, not to invade nor consent to invasion, nor to enslave any of that country and people, to whom we had guaranteed safety; that this he would enforce and defend until your majesty and the Governor Nuño de Guzmán, or the Viceroy in your name, should direct what would be most for the service of God and Your Highness.

When the children had been baptized, we departed for the town of San Miguel. So soon as we arrived, April 1, 1536, came Indians, who told us many people had come down from the mountains and were living in the vales; that they had made churches and crosses, doing all we had required. Each day we heard how these things were advancing to a full improvement.

Fifteen days of our residence having passed, Alcaraz got back with the Christians from the incursion, and they related to the captain the manner in which the Indians had come down and peopled the plain; that the towns were inhabited which had been tenantless and deserted, the residents, coming out to receive them with crosses in their hands, had taken them to their houses, giving of what they had, and the Christians had slept among them over night. They were surprised at a thing so novel; but, as the natives said they had been assured of safety, it was ordered that they should not be harmed, and the Christians took friendly leave of them.

NEW MEXICO'S NATIONAL PARKS

The following are descriptions of some of New Mexico's natural wonders.

Source: Robert Sterling Yard. <u>The Book of National Parks</u>. New York: Charles Scribner's Sons, 1919, pp. 370-374, 381-382.

The Spaniards found our semiarid southwest dotted thinly with the pueblos and its canyons hung with the cliff-dwellings of a large and fairly prosperous population of peace-loving Indians, who hunted the deer and the antelope, fished the rivers, and dry-farmed the mesas and valleys. Not so advanced in the arts of civilization as the people of the Mesa Verde, in Colorado, nevertheless their sense of form was patent in their architecture, and their family life, government, and religion were highly organized. They were worshippers of the sun. Each pueblo and outlying village was a political unit.

Let us first consider those national monuments which touch intimately the Spanish occupation.

GRAN QUIVIRA NATIONAL MONUMENT

Eighty miles southeast of Albuquerque, in the hollow of towering desert ranges, lies the arid country which Indian tradition calls the Accursed Lakes. Here, at the points of a large triangle, sprawl the ruins of three once flourishing pueblo cities, Abo, Cuaray, and Tabirá. Once, says tradition, streams flowed into lakes inhabited by great fish, and the valleys bloomed; it was an unfaithful wife who brought down the curse of God.

When the Spaniards came these cities were at the flood-tide of prosperity. Their combined population was large. Tabirá was chosen as the site of the mission whose priests should trudge the long desert trails and minister to all.

Undoubtedly, it was one of the most important of the early Spanish missions. The greater of the two churches was built of limestone, its outer walls six feet thick. It was a hundred and forty feet long and forty-eight feet wide. The present height of the walls is twenty-five feet.

The ancient community building adjoining the church, the main pueblo of Tabirá, has the outlines which are common to the prehistoric pueblos of the entire southwest and persist in general features in modern Indian architecture. The rooms are twelve to fifteen feet square, with ceilings eight or ten feet high. Doors connect the rooms, and the stories, of which there are three, are connected by ladders through trapdoors. It probably held a population of fifteen hundred. The pueblo has well stood the rack of time; the lesser buildings outside it have been reduced to mounds.

The people who built and inhabited these cities of the Accursed Lakes were of the now extinct Piro stock. The towns were discovered in 1581 by Francisco Banchez de Chamuscado. The first priest assigned to the field was Fray Francisco de San Miguel, this in 1598. The mission of Tabirá was founded by Francisco de Acevedo about 1628. The smaller church was built then; the great church was built in 1644, but was never fully finished. Between 1670 and 1675 all three native cities and their Spanish churches were wiped out by Apaches.

Charles F. Lummis, from whom some of these historical facts are quoted, has been at great pains to trace the wanderings of the Quivira myth. Bandelier mentions an ancient New Mexican Indian called Tio Juan Largo, who told a Spanish explorer about the middle of the eighteenth century that Quivira was Tabirá. Otherwise history is silent concerning the process by which the myth finally settled upon that historic city, far indeed from its authentic home in what now is Kansas. The fact stands, however, that as late as the latter half of the eighteenth century the name Tabirá appeared on the official map of New Mexico. When and how this name was lost and the famous ruined city with its Spanish churches accepted as Gran Quivira perhaps never will be definitely known.

"Mid-ocean is not more lonesome than the plains, nor night so gloomy as that dumb sunlight," wrote Lummis in 1893, approaching the Gran Quivira across the desert. "The brown grass is knee-deep, and even this shock gives a surprise in this hoof-obliterated land. The bands of antelope that drift, like cloud shadows, across the dun landscape suggest less of life than of the supernatural. The spell of the plains is a wondrous thing. At first it fascinates. Then it bewilders. At last it crushes. It is intangible but resistless; stronger than hope, reason, will—stronger than humanity. When one cannot otherwise escape the plains, one takes refuge in madness."

This is the setting of the "ghost city" of "ashen hues," that "wraith in pallid stone," the Gran Quivira.

EL MORRO NATIONAL MONUMENT

Due west from Albuquerque, New Mexico, not far from the Arizona boundary, El Morro National Monument conserves a mesa end of striking beauty upon whose cliffs are graven many inscriptions cut in passing by the Spanish and American explorers of more than two centuries. It is a historical record of unique value, the only extant memoranda of several expeditions, an invaluable detail in the history of many. It has helped trace obscure courses and has established important departures. To the tourist it brings home, as nothing else can, the realization of these grim romances of other days.

El Morro, the castle, is also called Inscription Rock. West of its steepled front, in the angle of a sharp bend in the mesa, is a large partly enclosed natural chamber, a refuge in storm. A spring here betrays the reason for El Morro's popularity among the explorers of a semidesert region. The old Zuñi trail bent from its course to touch this spring. Inscriptions are also found near the spring and on the outer side of the mesa facing the Zuñi Road.

For those acquainted with the story of Spanish exploration this national monument will have unique interest. To all it imparts a fascinating sense of the romance of those early days with which the large body of Americans have yet to become familiar. The popular story of this romantic period of American history, its poetry and its fiction remain to be written.

The oldest inscription is dated February 18, 1526. The name of Juan de Oñate, later founder of Santa Fe, is there under date of 1606, the year of his visit to the mouth of the Colorado River. One of the latest Spanish inscriptions is that of Don Diego de Vargas, who in 1692 reconquered the Indians who rebelled against Spanish authority in 1680.

The reservation also includes several important community houses of great antiquity, one of which perches safely upon the very top of El Morro rock.

Chaco Canyon National Monument

For fourteen miles, both sides of a New Mexican canyon sixty-five miles equidistant from Farmington and Gallup are lined with the ruins of very large and prosperous colonies of prehistoric people. Most of the buildings were pueblos, many of them containing between fifty and a hundred rooms; one, known to-day as Pueblo Bonito, must have contained twelve hundred rooms.

These ruins lie in their original desolation; little excavation, and no restoration has yet been done. Chaco Canyon must have been the centre of a very large population. For miles in all directions, particularly westward, pueblos are grouped as suburbs group near cities of to-day.

It is not surprising that so populous a desert neighborhood required extensive systems of irrigation. One of these is so well preserved that little more than the repair of a dam would be necessary to make it again effective.

PUEBLO LIFE IN NEW MEXICO

There follows a description of the
pueblos, the Indians who inhabit
them, along with their customs,
habits and ways of life.

Source: Clifton Johnson. <u>Highways and Byways of the
Rocky Mountains</u>. New York: The Macmillan Company,
1910, pp. 100-119.

MUCH of New Mexico seems to the casual observer a half-naked and stony wilderness where only the scantiest population can ever find subsistence. But there is a vast amount of good land that only needs irrigation to make it productive and beautiful; and by utilizing the streams fully and getting artesian water from below the surface the aspect of the region may be changed materially. By the time this possibility is realized to any marked extent the pueblo life now characteristic of a large portion of the country will be a memory of the past. Even as things are the picturesque conditions that make the Pueblo Indians and their villages so interesting are giving way to the white man's civilization, and their homes and habits are fast being modified.

Several of the pueblos are right on the line of the railroad. Of these, Laguna is perhaps best worth seeing, and moreover it is the point of departure for visiting Acoma, which in situation and in primitiveness is the most fascinating pueblo in all the Southwest. I made the fifteen mile journey from Laguna to Acoma in a light farm wagon accompanied by an Indian who served both as guide and driver. According to this Indian the road was a very good one; but I concluded he meant in comparison with others in the region. Sometimes we dragged slowly along through sand ruts, sometimes bumped over a rough shoulder of rock, and there were sudden gullies and steep hills, and stretches of hardened clay full of wheel tracks and hoof prints.

The scenery was rather forbidding. All about, at frequent intervals, rose the mesas with their flat tops and their sides strewn with boulders that had fallen from above. Some of them were mere hills, others mountainous in size and height. The half-barren land between was dotted with bushy cedars, very thick-stemmed at the ground, but soon tapering off, and always dwarfed in stature. At last we descended into a big level valley that looked like the floor of some old lake. It was thinly grassed, and numerous flocks of sheep, horses and cattle were grazing on it. Each flock of sheep included a number of black ones, and still more variety was added by the presence of several goats, which are valued not only for their milk, but as a protection to the sheep from wild animals. The coyotes follow the flocks of sheep very persistently, and the old goats stand guard, and fight the enemy, if necessary.

On ahead of us we could now see what is known as "The Enchanted Mesa," a vast castle-like rock rising with perpendicular walls from the floor of the plain to a height of four hundred and thirty feet. Its great size and ragged crags make it one of the most impressive natural wonders on the continent. Higher and higher it loomed as we drew nearer, and its name and the strange legends that have been told about it seemed quite in keeping with its peculiar character. According to one of the legends the pueblo of Acoma formerly occupied this height, and the path by which the people went up and down followed a crevice where a huge portion of the face of the precipice had partially separated from the main mass. One day, while all of the inhabitants except three sick women were at work in the fields on the plain below, there came a sudden storm, and the deluge of rain, or the lightning, sent the leaning ledge crashing down to the base of the mesa. The path was destroyed, and the three sick women perished beyond reach of aid on the then inaccessible cliff, and the rest of the community sought a new place for their village.

Several exploring parties in recent years have been to the summit of the great rock. The first of these, led by an Eastern college professor, laid siege to the mesa with a mortar and a number of miles of assorted ropes, supplemented by pulleys, a boatswain's chair and a pair of horses. Later parties have scaled the height aided only by a half dozen lengths of six foot ladders. They scrambled up a considerable portion of the distance over the loose stones at the sides of the precipice, and went still father up a narrow gorge. Presently the ladders became necessary, but only in one or two places did they have to put all six together. Nevertheless, the ascent was arduous, and at the steepest points somewhat perilous.

On top is an area of twelve acres that is almost bare rock. The explorers find there bits of broken pottery, stone axes and arrowheads, and ornaments made of wild hogs' tusks. The only indication of buildings is a regular arrangement of loose stones which evidently were the foundation of a round room. That the mesa was ever the site of a pueblo seems doubtful. More likely it was used simply as a place of refuge for small parties cut off from retreat to the main village by marauding enemies.

Three miles beyond, at the end of the valley on another wild mesa, is the pueblo of Acoma, a place of about half a thousand inhabitants. There it has been for seven hundred years, probably presenting from the beginning almost the identical appearance it does today. From a distance you would think the long continuous lines of adobe walls were a part of the mesa itself rising to a slightly greater height, but as you draw nearer you see occasional little chimneys and windows. The lofty table rock on which it stands is scarcely less romantic than the Enchanted Mesa, and the savage crags seem to have been carved by thunderbolts.

At first sight no way presents itself of climbing the precipitous sides; yet the Indians have no less than ten trails up different crevices, two of which are practical for horses. We, however, stopped with our team at one side of the mesa, where rose, here and there, isolated brown pillars and ledges—gigantic statues of nature's own making. About the base of them were rude cedar fences and a few hovels where the Indians kept their milch animals at night. Beside one of these corral clusters we unhitched our horses and put them in a hut. Then we ascended a sand drift that rose far up against the cliff; and when that ended clambered on up a narrow crevice which twisted this way and that, and sometimes passed over a strewing of boulders and sometimes beneath one lodged between the walls of the ravine. Steps had been rudely chipped out at the steepest points, and little pocket-like holes made in the adjoining cliff to grip with the hand.

The top of the mesa is a gentle slope of solid rock with a somewhat irregular surface. In two or three places are deep hollows where the rain water collects in little ponds, and this is the town's source of supply for drinking, cooking and washing. The water looked rather dubious, but I was assured that impurities settled to the bottom and left it clean and palatable.

A church and three parallel lines of homes constitute the village. Each series of homes rises in several terraces, and the ascent to the top of the first terrace is made by great rough outside ladders. To climb to the upper terraces, however, a few stone steps often do service. The original purpose of this type of architecture was protection against enemies; for the first story was without doors or windows, and when the ladders were drawn up the pueblos were safe from the assaults of their rudely armed, savage neighbors.

The walls are of stone laid in mud, and are daubed over smooth with mud inside, and frequently outside also. In constructing the roofs pine is used for the large beams, and across these cedar poles are laid close together. Next comes a layer of rushes and grass and the spiny leaves of the yucca. Then clay mud mixed with broken bits of wheat straw is put on. In a prolonged dry spell the roof is apt to crack, and unless the cracks are mended the rain soaks through and trickles down on the floor where it muddies up everything. Sheets of crystal gypsum serve for windows, the largest of which are about twelve by eighteen inches. They are windows of a single pane set solidly in an aperture of the wall.

The dwellings have from two to eight rooms, including such as are used for storage, and these are not nearly as gloomy as one might expect, for they are kept thoroughly whitewashed. One of the largest apartments is the living-room. It is warmed by a fireplace—not a very economical method of heating, perhaps; but the walls are so thick, and there is such lack of ventilation that a little fuel goes a long way. Wood is plentiful on the rough lands around, and the Indians can get all they want for the trouble of cutting and drawing it, or carrying it on their backs as they sometimes do. Scrub cedar is used chiefly, because that is most accessible; but pine is preferred when it can be had, for it burns with almost no smoke.

Across one end of the living-room a long pole is suspended from the rafters by thongs of rawhide. On this is hung all the extra clothing, blankets, belts, and some tanned buckskin not yet made into garments. Certain family heirlooms in the form of necklaces are likewise hung on the pole where they will attract the admiration of visitors. Some of these are very old and are made of fragments of seashells and black and cream colored stones shaped into beads. The best of them are worth fifteen or twenty horses.

A single sleeping apartment does for an entire family. The beds are mattresses of wool laid on the floor. There is never much circulation of air in the room, and if the weather is cold it is shut up tight and the fireplace furnishes the only ventilation. In warm weather, however, the Pueblo folk often sleep out on the terrace.

To descend to the lower rooms there is a trap-door and ladders. Climb down, and you find corn stored in a heap on the floor, and the wheat in big bins of plastered stone. Here, too, is the same sort of truck that white people usually relegate to the garret—broken tools and furniture, discarded clothing and whatever other useless things would be in the way in the upper rooms.

The young people are inclined to adopt white ways and to buy home conveniences that were formerly lacking. For instance, probably half the families now have tables; but it used to be the universal habit to eat on the floor, seated on a few little stools or blocks of wood, or blankets, while the bowls, platters and other pottery containing the food were distributed handily around.

The sanitary arrangements of the homes are not all they might be; yet the women sweep out daily, and there is an annual clean-up of the whole town when refuse and filth are carted off, walls whitewashed, and everything made as spick and span as the antique conditions of the town will allow.

In clothing, the Indians are gradually donning the garments of the whites, and so far as the men are concerned the transformation has often been complete. The elders of the tribe, however, still occasionally put on blankets and colored turbans. Blanket wearing is the rule with the women, but their gowns are of civilized cloth, and shoes and stockings are replacing the moccasins and leg-windings of buckskin. These buckskin leg-windings are supposed to have been devised as a protection against snakes, and the present-day wearers retain them as a matter of fashion. Yet, in summer, they find the buckskin so uncomfortably warm that they are apt to take it off and go barefoot.

The people are peaceful and thrifty. Those Indian tribes that roamed the mountains and plains have become wards of the government, but the Pueblo Indians have maintained a self-supporting integrity. They irrigate in the valleys, and raise such staples as corn and wheat, and a variety of garden vegetables, apples, plums and other fruit.

One of the picturesque incidents of the harvest is the wheat threshing. A level circle of ground is prepared with a surface of clay that is wet slightly and beaten and walked over till it is perfectly hard and smooth. After inclosing it with a fence of cedar poles, all the grain belonging to one farmer is arranged in the center in a big loose pile, probably not less than six yards in diameter, leaving about eight feet between it and the fence. The threshing is accomplished by driving a dozen or so horses around the circuit, beginning about nine in the morning. A squad of men and boys is on hand, armed with whips to chase the horses, and the central pile gradually works down so that all the ears are trodden out. By twelve o'clock the threshing is done, and in the afternoon the straw is thrown into a pile outside of the fence, and the wheat cleaned up and everything made ready for threshing the next man's crop on the morrow. The grain is separated from the chaff some windy day by throwing it up in the air with wooden shovels.

Dogs and poultry abound in the village; for every family keeps about a dozen fowls and very likely half that number of dogs. One may often meet an Indian on horseback with three or four curs ranging along in his wake. The Indians have great herds of sheep that wander among the mesas the year through, and they have many horses and cattle. Certain kinds of wild grass in the Southwest cure on the stalk, and this hay which nature furnishes, and nibblings of sagebrush and cactus keep the creatures from perishing in the lean months. The rainy season comes in July and August, after which the grass flourishes and there is abundance of feed through the fall. The only creatures that are provided with winter shelter are the horses and such cows and goats as are milked. For the horses rude stables are constructed, but the cows and goats get along with corrals. Alfalfa and oats are raised to feed these animals; and the corn fodder is saved and thrown up on the stable roofs to keep the stock from devouring it all at once or trampling it in the mire. The creatures get but scanty fare at best and are sure to be decidedly thin by spring. The sale of wool and of the sheep and other creatures is the chief source of the Indians' income. Something is added to this by the women who make pottery and dispose of it at the railway stations to travellers on the trains, or to traders; and a portion of the men work for wages.

A good deal of the money that comes into their hands is not spent wisely; but the same might be said of the expenditures of any class the world over. They gamble in a small way, buy candy and jewelry, cookstoves, sewing-machines, and brass bedsteads, and make curious misfits in introducing modern articles into their ancient homes and half savage habits of life.

Their amusements are more varied than the outsider would suspect, and, in particular, they enjoy races, both on foot and on horseback. One peculiar contest of speed and expertness consists in two rival parties going in opposite directions and each kicking a stick about a foot long and an inch in diameter over a course agreed on. This course may be anywhere from five to twenty miles long.

In the fall some day is fixed on for a rabbit hunt. The young men, to the number of about a score, ride off on horseback armed with clubs, which they hurl at every rabbit they sight. Each rider is eager to outdo his comrades and get the largest number, and they have a wild time chasing and heading off the rabbits. If fortune favors they may secure an average of two or three apiece, but on the other hand the whole crowd may kill only a half dozen.

A hunt of a more serious sort, yet scarcely less enjoyed, occurs in November, when three or four parties with about ten in each go off some fifty miles in different directions and camp and hunt deer.

For real fun, however, from the Indian viewpoint, nothing quite equals a special race it is customary to have on St. John's Day. The start is made on a level piece of ground near the village, where a live rooster has been buried in the sand all but its head. From fifteen to thirty racers mount their horses, go back from the rooster about two hundred yards, and at a signal put their steeds into a run. As they dash past the rooster each makes a grab at the bird until someone gets him. Then on they go in a mad rush engaged in a lively contest to gain possession of the captive chanticleer. The bird may change hands a number of times, and the fellow who brings him back to the starting-point is the victor.

After the harvest is finished dances are frequent until spring. Many of these dances are religious and commemorate some old tradition, and the participants dress up in all their barbaric glory. Other dances are merely social. There is not much movement in them. The dancers gather in a room and stand facing each other, one or two rows of men on this side, and similar rows of women on the other. Then they jump up and down, with certain changes of step, keeping time to the energetic music of drums and their own chanting.

One other pleasure that should be mentioned is the nutting expeditions. There are great forests of pines within twelve or fifteen miles, and thither the Indians resort in the late autumn and erect their tents on the mountain sides, a number of families grouped together, mostly women and children. They pick up thousands of bushels and have great sport. The nuts are nearly all consumed in the months to come by the Indians themselves. They like them best roasted, and evening is the favorite time for eating them. It is customary to set out the nuts when visitors happen in, and while those present feast they gossip and perhaps repeat the ancient folk tales of their race. They are great story-tellers, and some of the old men—especially certain of the numerous medicine men—are professionals in the art. The stories are a mingling of fact and fiction. Some of them have to do with long journeys and adventurous hunting excursions. Others are narratives of fights with the Navajos and of the deeds of the tribal heroes. These heroes are still human in their attributes if they lived within a generation or two, but before that they are demigods.

In the presence of white men the Indians are usually silent and undemonstrative, but among themselves they carry on much lively chatter that is both loquacious and humorous, and they will often stay up half the night over their small talk.

The climate is favorable to health; and now that the Indians are no longer swept off wholesale by small-pox, every hardy child has a fair prospect of a long life. Rheumatism, pneumonia, and diphtheria are perhaps the most prevalent diseases. The people have a good deal of faith in the curative properties of roots and herbs, and when these fail call in a medicine man. The physician tries to effect a cure by incantations; and he may resort to breathing on the patient or will use his eagle feathers to brush away the pain, or he will stroke the sick person with a bear's claw, which is another implement of his trade. Often his labors continue for hours at a time. His reward is generally a present of provisions or some article of clothing.

Each tribe has its governor and other officers, elected annually. The voting is done at a public meeting where the supporters of the rival candidates stand up in turn to be counted. In the evening, after the election, there is a big dance in some private house that has a large dining-room. It lasts most of the night. Once a month the council holds a session to transact public business and settle quarrels. This is a daytime meeting, and every official present receives a fee of fifty cents. Money for needful expenses comes largely from fines for drunkenness or assaults, but once in a while a small assessment is levied. Roads, bridges, fences, and irrigating ditches are taken care of by each man contributing a certain amount of labor on them yearly. All the land is owned in common, but any family can have set off to it as much as it will cultivate. If this land is allowed to lie idle for three years it reverts to the pueblo.

When the first Spaniards invaded the region the Pueblos seem to have accepted their rule and religion without any very strenuous resistance. But in 1681 a plot was formed to throw off the yoke. A day was set for the massacre of all Caucasians in the pueblo country. Four hundred persons including soldiers, civilians, and priests were killed, and the rest fled for their lives. Churches were pillaged and torn down and mines filled up. Three priests who were in Acoma at the time of the outbreak were taken to a high point on the edge of the mesa and compelled to jump. Two were thus killed outright, but the gown of the third expanded into a sort of parachute which broke the force of his fall and saved him from injury. The Indians thought his escape from death was due to heavenly intervention and they gave him his liberty.

It soon happened that the leader of the revolt, intoxicated by success, insisted on being paid divine honors. Hero worship of this sort was not to the liking of the rest of the Indians, and dissensions were a result. Besides, the different tribes got to squabbling among themselves. So in a dozen years the Spaniards had reconquered the pueblos. Since then they have been at peace with the whites, but have suffered much at the hands of the Navajos and Apaches. They are naturally peaceful, but they would fight hardily in defence of their homes; and when they were on the walls of their Gibraltar-like towns with their bows and arrows, lances and war-clubs they were by no means to be despised.

Their savage foes, therefore, confined their efforts to cutting off small parties and stealing sheep. Sometimes the Apaches would pick up a stray child. This child was made a member of the captor's tribe, and a good vigorous boy was always considered a welcome addition to the tribal strength.

The Pueblo Indians gave our own government valuable help in its operations against the nomadic Navajos, both in fighting and as scouts. Their natural capacity, energy, and thrift place them decidedly above the average of red men, and their homes and ways of life are strikingly original and interesting. This is especially true of Acoma which stands on its rugged mesa just as it has for centuries past, basking in the summer suns and swept by the winter blasts, with that wild region around of fantastic rocks, curiously eroded pillars and great buttes.

Another place in New Mexico possessing a peculiar attraction on account of its age is Sante Fe. It is the oldest European town in the United States, and it contains the oldest church and the oldest dwelling. These two structures adjoin each other and are impressive in their simplicity and evident antiquity. They are of thick-walled adobe, as are many other buildings in the town, which is as much Mexican as it is American in appearance and manners. It lies in a vast semi-arid basin with hills and lofty mountains at some distance. Little irrigating ditches network the town and there are luscious gardens and thriving trees. The inhabitants number only a few thousand and the place has much the character of a big lazy village. Its people like to loiter on the shadowy, green-turfed plaza and on the corridor-like sidewalks, across which the older buildings have extended pillared porticos. There has apparently never been any regular plan in the building of the city, and the streets wind, and zigzag, and jerk around corners in a most unexpected fashion. As a somewhat garrulous visitor whom I fell in with remarked: "You walk along and think you are going somewhere only to find you are going somewhere else. Oh, it's jiggety jog; but, by gracious! I like it."

The speaker was a gray old man who had been a captain in the Civil War. Sante Fe's reputation as a health resort had drawn him thither, and he was delighted with its climate, its quaintness and the friendliness of its inhabitants. He had a cheerful greeting for everyone we met. Often he paused to shake hands with this one or that—to sympathize with a sick man, to pat a child on the head, to discuss history and religion with some priest.

"You couldn't use street cars here," he said in continuing his comments on the character of the town, "unless they were made on an angle and a circle, because the streets are so crooked. Why, there isn't a square corner in the city. You go along one street, and you run right up ag'in' a house. You try another and it takes you into a dooryard; and I was in one that ended like a wedge so I just had to turn around and come back.

"See those little burros with the loads of wood on their backs," said the captain pointing down the street with his cane. "The wood is all cut up ready for the stove, and the driver in charge peddles it from house to house. Each burro carries about two wheelbarrow loads, and they've come anywhere from five to twenty miles. A man or boy follows behind and tickles them up with a switch—any old way to get there.

"But those peddlers are making an honest living. I recall back in Ohio a man who went around with a two-horse covered wagon, and on the sides was painted in big letters 'WHAT IS IT? Admission 10 cents.' The fellow lived in the wagon and drove from place to place exhibiting an animal he had inside. You paid your ten cents and went up some steps behind, and when you saw the creature you'd say: 'Why, it looks like a ground-hog,' and that's what it was—nothing but a dirty Oregon ground-hog. And yet that man stirred up curiosity by his sign, and people would climb into his wagon and discuss and discuss what the animal really was. I suppose if I was to attempt a thing like that the sheriff would get me sure and put me in a lunatic asylum. But tricks go all right with some men."

A wayside shrub attracted my companion's attention, and he broke off a twig, which he showed to the next man we met with a query as to its name. The man replied rather gruffly that he didn't know what the shrub was and didn't care.

"You don't live in this town, I guess," commented the captain, and the man shook his head and walked on.

"I knew he didn't," the captain declared, "or he wouldn't have answered a civil question like that. They're a fine people here, polite and intelligent and accommodating, and they have the best climate in the world. Back in Ohio it's an old saying that we have six months of winter and three months of late in the fall every year. But here, even in winter, most of the days are pleasant and comfortable. Then in summer, though the thermometer goes up as high as one hundred and twenty in the shade, they tell me it is a dry heat that don't trouble a person. A man may perspire, and a few drops fall from his face, but he don't get wringing wet as he would in the East. It's healthy here. You bet it is; and I never was anywhere that suited me better."

So he went on in his own lively fashion expatiating on the charms of the old town, and in his opinion it evidently was not much inferior to the original Garden of Eden.

NOTE.—New Mexico, in spite of its general aspect of arid and sunburned monotony, has much to entice the traveller to pause and observe it more in detail; but of its various attractions the pueblos are the most piquant and unusual. Some of these are very easy of access, though naturally such are less characteristic than those more remote. The many-chambered communal homes in the territory number over a score, and their inhabitants own nearly a million acres of land. Albuquerque is a good central point from which to start visiting the pueblos. Isleta, one of the most important, is only ten miles distant, right on the railroad. Laguna is fifty-six miles farther to the west, and is not only extremely interesting in itself, but is the nearest point of departure from the railway for Acoma and the Enchanted Mesa. Accommodations at Laguna are poor, but the trip to Acoma will amply reward one for a good deal of discomfort. The journey to it and back can easily be made in a day. Another noteworthy pueblo is Zuni, forty-five miles from Fort Wingate.

For enjoyment of a different sort visit old Santa Fe. It offers exceptional attractions in the way of climate, quaintness, age, historic associations, and excellent hotels. The town is only a few miles off the main line of east and west railroad, and merits much more attention from travellers than it has had hitherto.

Still another attraction of New Mexico is its weather. The typical day is absolutely cloudless, and the sun makes its journey across the vast blue dome of the sky without the least film of mist to obscure its brightness, and they have three hundred such days every year.

NEW MEXICO: TERRAIN AND WILD LIFE

The description of New Mexico presented here gives a fine picture of the rugged beauty of the state along with a fine description of the wild life of the area. In addition interesting anecdotes of the voyage are presented.

Source: Paul Fountain. <u>Eleven Eaglets of the West</u>. New York: E. P. Dutton, 1906.

PASSING round the base of Ute Peak, an isolated mount 10,000 feet high, we struck the course of the Rio Grande, and moved southward, making for Santa Fé, where we intended to rest for a short time. The country passed through was somewhat dreary, timber appearing to be even more scanty than in Colorado; and the reddish and yellowish rocks were exceedingly arid. Stunted poplars (cotton-wood), aspen, a sort of evergreen oak, and cedar were the only trees recognised, and these were scattered on the face of the hills in a very meagre way. Cacti, of which we had seen traces in the northern terrritory, here rapidly, as we moved south, became a characteristic vegetable genus of the land; and agaves were also seen, together with a few plants and shrubs, which I thought it probable had been introduced from the eastern side of the Continent by the agency of man.

Although it was still quite early in the fall, as we approached Santa Fé, a sharp shower of mingled sleet and snow fell. It did not lie on the ground, but the opinion of all of us was that the weather was much colder here than in the land we had just left.

Santa Fé is the oldest city in the West; and the inhabitants claim that it is the oldest in North America.

Like many other old towns of Spanish origin in the United States, it is an exceedingly sleepy place: and during the 350 years it has been in existence, so far from making progress has it been, that it has actually greatly retrograded. This is strange, because for many years it has been an important place, the great trail from St Louis to Santa Fé being one of the best known and most used in the United States. Annually there came hither a train of from 300 to 400 waggons, travelling overland: a fleet of prairie schooners, in fact, besides many independent individuals who, like myself, chose their own route, and faced their own risks.. As the merchandise brought by these waggons was distributed from Santa Fé, and there were moreover several go-a-head American firms trading in the city, it is passing strange that it has never shaken off its sloth and got upon its feet. But it is so with all the towns of Spanish foundation. Perhaps I had better say Spanish-American towns, which I have visited, for doubtless some of my critical friends are well able to correct me, and will show that places I think to be of "Citizen" *make* are really born of the haughty Don.

There is something in the very air of Santa Fé which is seductive, and provocative of indolence; and I soon began to feel that it would be dangerous for me to prolong my stay there. There is a good deal of Spanish blood still in the place; and I saw more than one handsome dark-eyed girl glancing from the balconies at me with coy, but coquettish, curiosity; and others were passed in the streets. Many of them, perhaps, like the men, are Mexicans; but they seemed to me to be prettier than the average Mexican women, and to more nearly resemble the Rio Janeiro beauties with whom I was, at a later period, so charmed.

They wear short skirts, displaying splendidly developed and shapely ankles; while the ladies of Brazil adopt long and trailing dresses. Of course, they are of different nationality: but really the difference between a Spaniard and a Portuguese is no greater than that between a Yorkshireman and a West-countryman.

The houses of Santa Fé are built of stone in a few cases, but far more generally of a kind of brick, which has not been burnt, but has been hardened by exposure to the sun. Many of them are provided with galleries, or balconies, and the style of architecture is that found in all Spanish towns, viz. blank walls, with latticed doors and few and narrow windows toward the street. There are, in some instances, considerable pieces of ground enclosed with the houses; the houses are well detached from one another; and the streets, long, crooked, narrow, rambling, full of sly-looking corners, suggestive of clandestine meetings and jealous lovers lurking with hateful stiletto in hand—instances of which acts are by no means uncommon, even now.

The old palace, in which the first Spanish governors of the territory resided, still remains apparently entirely unaltered, or meddled with, in recent days: an instance of conservatism which does high honour to the care and good taste of the United States officials. I did not go over the building, and there is nothing very striking on its exterior.

The population is only some 4000 or 5000 persons. It is asserted that in the palmy days of the overland route, it rose as high as 9000 or 10,000, but that prosperity did not last, and it rapidly sank again. There is, however, a floating population, so to speak; and occasionally there are many hundreds of miners congregated in the city; but probably Santa Fé will never be a very important place. It is situated at a considerable elevation above the sea, in a park similar to those of Colorado, but less fertile and not so flat. The surrounding mountains are some of the highest in the territory, which is essentially a mining country; the ranching interest, at this time, not being worth mention.

Continuing the journey south, we were much struck with the similarity of the scenery to the deserts of California and Oregon. It is of the wildest description; vast broken rocks alternating with patches of saline desert, sandy plain, and lava lakes. Although several great rivers run down the territory, water is scarcer in some districts of New Mexico than in any other part of the West we traversed, and we often suffered much from an insufficient supply. The lakes in this part of the country seem to be all what are locally called " soda ponds," though many of them are saline. The brooks also are strongly impregnated with various salts, and after very short courses sink into the ground.

With the exception of three or four kinds to be mentioned presently, the land is almost destitute of mammals and birds; and other forms of life are all scarce compared with the countries previously described. Therefore I had some difficulty in following my own advice, and watching the flight of birds towards water. The birds, truly, were seen; but the distance they evidently had to go to reach the much-desired element was so great that we could not follow. One of the best plans I found in practice here was to give the horses their head and let them choose their own road. Horses (these wilderness-bred animals, at any rate) evidently can smell water a goodly distance; and we several times found springs by following their guidance, though this sometimes took us out of our way.

Hundreds of travellers are known to have perished in these deserts; but I stick to my text that they need not, in most of the cases, have done so. Our own plight was, more than once, perhaps as desperate as that of any men who ever crossed this region. Great relief was obtained, and the lives of the horses probably saved, by using the sliced leaves of cacti and agaves, as well as the fruit of the former. By pressing the leaves an abundant supply of refreshing and exceedingly wholesome juice can be obtained. The prickles must be removed before horses can be fed on the sliced leaves; and this is a wearisome job, but that can scarcely be complained of when life is at stake. The leaves of the agave are thick and fleshy, and full of juice, and afford excellent fodder as well as drink, and, together with the leaves or stems and fruit of cacti, are one of the best febrifuges to be found in the country.

In the south of the territory the candle, or candelabrum, plant (*Cereus gigantia*) is abundant. This species of cactus grows to the height of at least 40 feet here; but in the adjoining territory of Arizona, I have seen them nearly 30 feet taller. They grow upright, looking, when not branched, like tall posts: hence I suppose the name of "The Staked Plains" given to ground covered with them. The Staked Plains are in Texas, but they enter the south-east corner of New Mexico. When the plant (it may almost be termed a tree) is branched, its singular right-angled arms stand up parallel with the trunk like the branches of a candelabrum. A plain covered with these singular cacti, which sometimes grow pretty thickly together, is a singular, and, at evening time, a weird sight. Several species of small birds build their nests in the forked arms of these cacti, absolutely secure from all terrestrial enemies, for no animal or snake dare ignore the mighty prickles of this plant.

The *cereus gigantia* bears a fruit which is a bright green colour externally, smooth, oval in shape, and about the size of a goose's egg. If not exactly delicious, the crimson-coloured pulp of this cactus-apple is most refreshing as well as nutritious. As it is impossible to climb the plant, and ladders are not usually found in the desert, the only way of obtaining this fruit is to poke it off with a long stick. It can be eaten either raw or cooked, and is perhaps preferable in the latter condition.

Besides this cactus, there are others which yield excellent fruits, generally about the size of a filbert, and there is also a species of prickly pear in some parts of the country. The flowers of many kinds are exceedingly handsome and curious, some a bright red, others a pure white. And another curious plant in these southern deserts is the "Bayonet-tree," a species of zucca, so called from the sharp knife-like leaves, which are capable of inflicting a nasty wound if accidentally run against or incautiously handled. Some of these plants have a singular appearance owing to a fringe of hair-like filaments hanging down from the edges of the leaves. The Indians use these filaments for sewing and tying purposes, and even twist them into a cord or small rope. Some of this rope which I obtained was found to be of great strength and very durable. I have since learned that this fibre has become an article of great use to civilised men : let me hope that they will use it with discretion, and not work it off the face of the earth, as they have so many useful creations great and small.

The above are the most characteristic and curious

members of the vegetable kingdom found in New Mexico. Of lesser plants there are many which, no doubt, would interest a botanist, and not less so a lover of Nature; but much space cannot be devoted to descriptions of plants of which I cannot give the specific names. There is a marked difference between New Mexico and Colorado in this respect at least, that, while the more northern territory abounds with beautiful flowering plants, this class of herbage is very deficient in southern landscapes. Yet there are, in places, flowers both singular and beautiful. One remarkable but inconspicuous weed deserves notice as it seems to be a kind of fly-trap. The stems exude a sticky, tenacious fluid, which holds fast and speedily kills any insect pitching on or flying against it. Many of the weeds were covered with flies and beetles, which had been unfortunate enough to come near this sticky trap. Perhaps they are allured, for on putting a piece of the weed against the tongue, I found that it had a distinctly sweet taste. Flies as large as a humble-bee were caught in the toils of this plant, which does not grow above a foot or 15 inches in height, is not abundant, and is, apparently, very local: for I found it only in a confined area south of the Gallinos Creek, a tributary of the Pecas River.

Several kinds of snakes infest these desert regions; and though they may not be often seen by persons travelling straight across the country, naturalists searching among the rocks, etc., may run considerable risk, and it is as well to have some weapon in the hand when searching broken ground, or among herbage. I used to carry a scythe, fastened to a straight pole, and sharpened on both edges, a most formidable weapon, similar to those with which the Poles had tickled their

Russian tyrants a few years previously. In the hands of a strong man this weapon is good enough to face a grizzly with, for no animal whatever could stand against its terrible sweeping cut, or equally deadly thrust, while such creatures as rattlesnakes, and similar vermin, are instantly disabled, if suddenly come upon.

The common deer, as we may call the white-tailed species, prongbuck, and wipiti, are said to be found in New Mexico; but we did not see any deer at all within the bounds of the territory. They are probably seldom found south of the northern Parks and mountains. The chief animals we did meet with were skunks, coyotes, badgers, hares, and minks.

The skunks were not plentiful, being seen three or four times only: but this animal was met with in Wyoming and Colorado, where it seems to frequent certain tracts in particular. Here, one was found under the waggon one night trying to climb up to a couple of recently killed hares. On being disturbed it attempted to run away, but was killed by one of the dogs. In dying it emitted its filthy odour, but the dog was not sprinkled: they never are, according to my experience; and the assertion that dogs will not attack skunks is absolute nonsense. I have seen scores killed, and known men to keep dogs for the express purpose of hunting them. If the odour is intended by Nature as a protection to the animal, it most signally fails of its purpose.

The skunk killed was a young one; but the full-grown animals, while without doubt of the same species (*Mephitis mephitica*), seemed to be under-sized. On the other hand, a badger, which was seen the next day, was an unusually fine animal. Observing certain markings on it which led me to think that it might be a new species, I tried to find it; and, while searching the holes and clefts in the rocks, I disturbed a whole family of skunks, which seemed to consist of the parents and five half-grown cubs.

The badger was not found, but subsequently, in the southern part of the territory, the animal was found to be abundant, and I obtained several skins. The only difference I could perceive between it and the common badger was that this New Mexican animal had an irregular white stripe down the middle of the back. It may be considered, I think, a local variety. It was probably frequently seen further north while I was watching at night, but mistaken, in the gloom, for some unknown animal.

The mink was seen only once, at the head of Mintado Creek, where it occupies the rocky gorge, a spot remarkable for its deep, quiet pools. There is rich herbage here, but very few bushes or trees; and the little animals, which are about 16 inches long, exclusive of the tail, which is another 6 or 7 inches, greatly resemble minute otters. They are of a dark reddish-brown colour, the fur resembling velvet in appearance.

Coyotes are numerous, and the hares exceedingly so. They are found almost everywhere, but most abundantly in the Parks. These hares, called rabbits throughout the West, are, considered as food, dry and flavourless; but they nevertheless afforded us an agreeable change in a country where fresh meat is rarely obtainable.

The coyotes are bolder here than in any other district where I have met with them; and though they are, on the whole, of nocturnal habits, they are often seen about during the day, and always, in numbers, early in the evening. Small animals and birds, killed for food, used to be hung on the side of the waggon until wanted;

and when the horses were hobbled and turned loose to graze, the men would saunter about the country to smoke and amuse themselves, leaving our travelling home unattended and unwatched. On one of these occasions I was sitting inside, quietly writing at the little folding table used for that purpose, when my attention was attracted by a slight noise. Cautiously looking out at the window, I saw three or four coyotes sneaking round and under the waggon; and one of the number was making frantic efforts to reach some game hanging at the side, springing and endeavouring to help himself up with his paws. The attitudes and movements of the little animal were most graceful, and I watched it with great interest, noting that it sprang upward a sheer 6 feet at least. At length it contrived to grab the nose of a suspended hare, hanging on by its teeth for several moments, while it tried to scramble up the vertical sides of the waggon, shaking the hare meanwhile to disengage it. Not succeeding in this, it was obliged to release its hold, and drop back to the ground. But it continued its exertions, assisted by two of its companions, and at length tore down a duck, which was ready plucked and destined for supper. Thinking it time then to interfere for the protection of my property, I rushed to the door; but before I could seize a gun, and get out of the waggon, the coyotes had disappeared, and the duck with them.

After that we were somewhat troubled at night-time by these animals, which came prowling about to see what they could pick up. They must have followed the waggon, for this continued for three days, and a distance of fully 50 miles. It is the only occasion on which anything of the kind occurred with coyotes, though often I have known the common wolf to follow the waggon for more than a week, the howling of a couple of dozen of these animals being sometimes such a nuisance that I have arisen in the middle of the night, and fired a chance shot at them, which was a hint they were never slow to take, though when starving they would appear night after night, always keeping at such a distance that they could not be seen. At such times they would eat scraps left on the ground, but were still too wideawake to be trapped. Very rarely have I succeeded in trapping wolves. But this is a digression, for no common wolves were seen in New Mexico.

Needless to say, in all the States herein described I met with thousands of animals of all classes which cannot even be named without turning the book into a mere catalogue. Only when there is something uncommon to note can the animal life of the country be referred to; and here I may notice a class of creatures which seldom come under the observation of a traveller, or, at least, are thought worthy of half a page.

Looking at the arid wastes of this land, its hard-looking, bare, and sun-baked rocks, its want of vegetation and lack of all kinds of moisture, one would think the plains of New Mexico as unlikely a place for the habitat of slugs and snails as the desert of Sahara; nevertheless there is a very curious little slug found here, and that on the borders of saline lakes and pools of all spots. This, I think, is extraordinary, considering that salt is the most deadly of poisons to all land molluscs.

These slugs have a bluish line running down each side of the body, and a row of spots; and, as might be expected from the character of their habitat, are dry and hard to an unusual degree for their family. They are very small, not an inch long, are found five or six together under stones; and at night come forth and climb to the very summit of weeds 4 or 5 feet high, where they feed on the buds.

It is almost as remarkable that there are snails of considerable size in the bare deserts, and that in the apparently driest spots. These may be found hiding in the tufts of hay-like grass. Another species is found under the sage-bushes, and yet another, a very small one this, on the giant cactus. There are snails in all parts of the West, some of them with handsomely shaped or coloured shells.

Birds are scarce in New Mexico. What species occur are found also in Arizona, and will be noticed in the account of that territory.

The Rio Grande del Norte of American geographers, Rio Bravo del Norte of the Mexicans, and plain Rio Grande of the people of the land (Rio being pronounced río by Americans) is the largest river in New Mexico, and runs in a tolerably straight course right down the territory, yet only a small portion of its entire course is within the State bounds. For the Rio Grande is nearly 2000 miles in length, though, for such a course, it is the most fiddling river in America. Within the boundary lines of the territory it generally runs in cañons of great depth with vertical, or nearly vertical, walls; but in view of the much that has been written about cañons, and what I must yet say of the mighty chasms of the Colorado, the natural features of the Grande will be passed by. The body of water in its channel is never in any degree proportionate to its length and breadth, and it is not navigable within the territory, nor, indeed, anywhere but on its lower reaches. I have seen some places almost dry, and it is fordable with ease at innumerable spots when the water is low; yet in due season there are mighty rushes of water, the product of melting snow, or storms, up the country. Then should any unfortunate traveller be caught in a portion of the cañon where the enclosing walls render an immediate escape impossible, his fate is assured. He may hear the roar of the oncoming waters for twenty minutes, or half an hour, before they actually reach him, for they swirl, twist, and evolve huge curling waves, with cruel slowness but overwhelming force, and the wretched man is not drowned but ground to fragments by the violence with which he is dashed against and swept over the ragged rocks in the bed of the river.

The sight of a sudden torrent in the Rio Grande is one of the most appalling scenes on the American continent. It is grand, no doubt, but too terrifically so to be witnessed altogether with equanimity. Possibly the sight, as we saw it, is of rare occurrence, or only to be seen at certain of the narrowest gorges of the cañon: for there were people in the region, knowing the river well, who had never witnessed such a display of furious force as that I described; yet I certainly did not exaggerate, and whatever may be said about the usual state of the current I had proof on other occasions that the rise of the river is sometimes very sudden. Huge blocks of rock were moved freely; in some cases masses 60 or 70 feet long and 30 broad were turned completely over. Some miners from Manzano afterwards reported that there had been a cloud-burst in the north, and there was much talk about it, proving that such visitations were not of common occurrence. This probably was the cause of the sudden flood. Two days afterwards, 20 miles lower down, we forded the river with ease! It is certain that a river which rises and falls with such extreme rapidity can never be navigated.

The course of the Rio Grande in the lower part of the territory is extremely tortuous. It doubles and loops almost as much as the Mississippi, and this must be the reason of the slow advance of freshets, and perhaps a sudden flood is, to some extent, jammed by the character of the course. The cliffs and country near the river are among the most destitute of vegetation of any in the territory; there is, however, plenty of grass, and it has been proved that the ground only wants irrigating to make it as fertile as any to be found in a western State. Unfortunately, the rivers all lie so deep that they are almost worthless for irrigation purposes.

In spite of all drawbacks there were indications that the valley (if it may be so called) of the Grande would become a chief centre of population. There was already a fair sprinkling of ranches, farms, and young towns—some of them youthful in population only, for they were founded by the Spaniards, and can boast of an antiquity of two or three hundred years; which, in the United States, is very ancient indeed. Sheep and cattle are raised here, the former especially. The ground is only cultivated under exceptional circumstances, and in very limited areas.

Proceeding westward, we passed over some very solitary tracts, where for hundreds of miles we saw no indications whatever of our fellow-men. The first people met in this district were some Indians, who were friendly, as they mostly are in this territory, although they belong to warlike tribes, who in former days completely mastered their Spanish conquerors, and compelled them to give complete freedom to the native tribes, granting them release from labour in the mines, and from tribute. In fact they drove the Spaniards out of the towns and forts and held uncontrolled possession of the country for a period of nearly twenty years, during which they destroyed all mine shafts, and many other works of the whites. The territory was, at the time of the journey under description, far more populous than either Wyoming or Colorado; but I did not learn the numbers. The Indians are a very few thousands in number, and are found mostly in the east, in the Staked Plains region, and in the west, the presence of whites in the north and middle of the territory having probably driven them to the frontiers.

As we left the desert plains and advanced towards the mountains we found ourselves once more in the midst of dense forests, an experience we had not had since quitting Wyoming; and the trees, too, were of a size and height such as we had seldom seen since leaving the Coast States.

On the lowest of the foot-hills the giant cacti grew in such numbers that they shut out from sight the country ahead, and had the appearance of a forest. They were really always some feet apart, never growing sufficiently close to choke each other, as forest trees often do; and they so appropriate all the moisture of the ground that no trees or bushes can find sustenance near them. Here they were in all stages of growth, some 50 feet high, others just appearing above the ground as a rounded, prickly mass, which it is most dangerous to tread upon. The spines will seriously lame a horse, and they seem to poison a wound, in spite of the absolute wholesomeness of the plant itself. At any rate, I have seen men and horses with greatly inflamed wounds from pricks of these spines.

After clearing the cactus woods exclusive, we found plants of this class scattered among pines and other hard-wood trees. On what may be called the hills in contradistinction to the mountains, we found many trees that were familiar to us: cedar, oak, tamarack, hickory, with the ubiquitous poplar and aspen. The mountains were covered here, in the west, to the very summits, with pines of noble size and proportions—120 to 150 feet high—pigmies compared with the giants of the Coast ranges; but yet far finer trees than any we had of late met with.

Still, even in these forests, mammals and birds were remarkably scarce in species, though the individuals of some kinds were very numerous. Hares, for instance, almost swarmed, and badgers were plentiful. The coyotes were abundant enough in the plains, and on the foot-hills, but few were seen on higher ground.

Almost nightly, small birds congregated near the waggon when we camped for the night, though few might have been seen during the day. They also appeared in the morning, being tame enough to perch on the top of the waggon, and hop about the horses' hoofs. They consisted of several species of tits, wrens, and warblers, and similar little creatures, known to the men mostly by such popular names as desert-sparrows, tree-sparrows, peewees, chippies, etc., etc. These birds all retire at an early hour. The moment we halted and began to hobble the horses, they would appear, one or two at a time, till we had several dozen around us, but they all went again before the sun had set. Struck by the regularity of the retirement, I paid particular attention to their movements. A few would linger until the sun touched the horizon, but before it had sunk completely out of sight, every one had disappeared. Not a single small bird could be found during twilight.

In the morning the first to appear was a graceful little thing about the size of a wagtail, and something like one in habit and appearance, called by the men a bobtail. This was followed by the "sparrows" and tits, the wrens coming last. These last, and the tits, were as fond of a piece of fat meat, or of picking a bone, as their namesakes are said to be in Europe; but the chief objects of search were the crumbs and broken food dropped on the ground. This seems a strange taste for desert birds which cannot find bread or biscuit except under the most exceptional circumstances. When they get the chance, however, they devour crumbs of all sorts of cooked food with avidity.

While small birds nearly all disappear with the sun, others only appear with the moon and stars. Of these I had but the scantiest opportunities of ascertaining the species. A large brown hawk was often seen hovering over the forest at a great height, but I could never get near enough to ascertain the species. In the forest itself the trees grew so thickly together and the gloom was so intense, especially at evening time, that very little could be learned within its shades. It was, however, occupied by owls and some kind of goat sucker, which had a different cry to any other I have heard. It sounded like the words, uttered slowly, "Whop-whop-whir-whop!" and then very fast, "Tshir-tshir-tshir-tshir-r-r-r-r-whop!" This bird was exceedingly shy, so that all my efforts to catch a glimpse of it were exerted in vain.

Often, before lying down for the night, I would saunter some distance from the camp fire, to meditate and listen: for I love the sounds of the desert, however few and feeble they may be; and the odours of the night air in these glorious wilds are always delicious, and a looked-for enjoyment at the close of the day.

It is a peculiar sensation to stand alone in a solitary

land, with, as far as one knows, no other human being within hundreds of miles, and darkness on all sides. The sense of loneliness is overcoming: and, if indeed the human race sprang from a single pair, it is surprising that our first ancestors retained their reason. I am exceptionally constituted myself, inasmuch as I love solitude, and can endure it, in comparison with what I have noted in other men, to an extraordinary degree; but the absolute solitude of a lone land could not be endured by any person, I feel convinced, for a prolonged period without inducing a diseased condition of the mental faculties. Robinson Crusoe is a delightful fiction; but twenty years on a solitary island! Would it not end in insanity before a fourth of that period had expired? Yet in one point I can confirm the truthfulness to Nature of Defoe's charming story. *Solitaires* always evince a great liking for pets, and deprived of the society of their own race, invariably seek that of the subject animals. Robinson Crusoe without his monkey and his parrot would not be Robinson Crusoe.

But the solitary night-watcher on the plains. Let him keep still and listen. Those sounds which are in his immediate neighbourhood will probably be the first to attract his attention. That whirring, buzzing sound reminds him of the cockchafers he pursued when a boy, and treated so cruelly. The sound here comes from a cloud of beetles, though not cockchafers, which fly by night; and he will probably get a sharp rap or two on the face from the blundering things. These beetles appear in great numbers after dark, flying low, and making a combined hum, which may be heard a distance of several hundred yards.

There are other insect noises, the sharpest and most predominant of which is the chirping of the kittydads and field-crickets which swarm on the plains, especially where the ground rises into gently-sloped hills of a few hundred feet in height. These creatures keep up their calls till about one o'clock in the morning, at which hour the coolness of the air becomes very keen, and they probably retire to their holes to avoid the cold.

A murmuring, half-frightened, half-complaining sort of chatter is that of some roosting bird, which has been disturbed by your passage near the bush where it is resting; while the distant bark, which seems to be more than a mile off, and is only faintly heard, is that of a dog-coyote; and if you listen carefully you will presently hear an answering bark, very different in intonation from the first, of the female who is answering his challenge.

Possibly a startled cry, a scream, a roar of agonised fright, may reach your ear, and you may know that the prowling puma has made a successful pounce upon some unwary victim; and if you have courage enough to silently creep forward, and the wind is in your favour, you may presently get near enough to hear a soft, flabby, tearing sound, and you will know that the great cat is stripping from the bones the warm flesh still full of wet blood. If you hear the sharp sound of crunching bones, you will know that it is a bear, and not a puma, which is feasting; and you will probably not care to stop to listen to the complaining grunts and snuffles to which Bruin always gives vent when eating. The large marrow bones are always eagerly sought by a bear, and he will crush them between his molars as soon as he can strip the flesh from them and get them between his jaws. Then you will hear him suck, suck, suck, with a smacking of the lips, like some vulgar yokel over his beans and bacon. You had better not stop too long, though: for Bruin is jealous of interruption when feeding, and this is a time when he is particularly likely to attack an intruding human being.

These are some of the night sounds which a silent listener is likely to hear, and will give hint enough that there is much in the wilderness, even in the darkest hours of the daily revolution, to interest the observant lover of Nature. He may very possibly meet with *sights* too, especially in districts which have not been much disturbed by hunters, in the form of dark shadows stealing stealthily past him. On some of these night watches I have had both bears and pumas pass within a very few yards of me, apparently surveying so curious an animal as man with astonishment, and pondering whether such a singular-looking creature was worth sampling. Apparently "the answer was in the negative," to use what seems to have become a parliamentary term, for I was never attacked on these occasions: and, on the other hand, I never became the aggressor. For shooting dangerous animals, at all times a risky business, becomes a doubly ticklish affair when there is not sufficient light to make the marksman tolerably sure of his aim.

In many parts of this territory hot springs abound. I was often asked by ranchmen and shepherds if I had seen this or that locally famous fountain; but the first I actually came across was on the western borders near Corduroy Cañon. It was an intermittent spring, the water lying deep in a circular hole, from which it bubbled up every few minutes, but with irregular intervals. Several other hot springs were found a few miles further north.

While in this neighbourhood we met a herd of cattle being driven from pasture to pasture, a common practice in the West, and shared a fat beast with the boys. A quarter of beef being placed on the top of the waggon for the night, previously to drying, in the morning I found a couple of blue-jays worrying away at the particles of fat, and enjoying a delicious feast. They flew away on my appearance, but soon came back, and remained fluttering backwards and forwards until the horses were put to the waggon in preparation for departure.

The birds were not the common blue-jays, but the *Cyanocitta mocrolopha* of the museums. It is a very common bird in the Coast States, and was from time to time seen in all the South Central States; and it is one of those little creatures which cannot fail to greatly interest the true naturalist, on account of its bold and lively habits. It seems to be gifted with a considerable degree of inquisitiveness, and it would sometimes spend hours examining the waggon, and has even entered it when no one has been by, and flown off with such morsels of food as it could secure. On one occasion a bird of this kind attempted to fly off with a pocket-handkerchief, doubtless to incorporate it in its nest, but the task proved to be beyond its strength. The bird is fond of playing with rags, and will fly off with such scraps of linen and paper as it can secure. A young bird which I kept for a long time would amuse itself by pulling about any pieces of rag it could find; and would attempt to tug the handkerchief from the breast-pocket of my shirt. It never hid things like the magpie, but made quite a collection of such articles as pens, pencils, thimbles, percussion caps (which it obtained by wrenching open a leather pouch), pins, needles, pieces of paper, threads, hair, feathers, etc.: some of which it found about the waggon, and others were brought in from outside; for it had its liberty, and a favourite perch with it was on the back of one particular horse, and at other times it took up its position on the half door at the front of the waggon, and chattered and screamed by the hour at a time. It was sometimes very noisy, and learned to whistle like the boys, and make a number of sounds which were evidently intended to imitate those which had attracted its attention. It was intelligent and familiar, and would fly 50 or 60 yards to meet me when I approached the waggon, and often hopped from boy to boy among the men. It did not like to be handled, but if not touched would often take a perch on my shoulder. It lived about eighteen months, and died suddenly, from no apparent cause.

The plumage of this jay is of a brownish-black colour, finely mottled and marked with light blue, and it is remarkable for its helmet-shaped crest. In a wild state it is at first somewhat cautious, but if not persecuted it becomes as bold and familiar as an English house-sparrow.

Among the mountains of the western side of New Mexico, as in those of other parts of the territory, there are many pretty Parks of small size. Most of them are well wooded, and not a few are quite fairy haunts, being a tangle of beautifully-foliaged and blossoming shrubs. Here I found violets of a yellow colour, and without scent.

These tangles, I discovered, were favourite haunts of a number of pretty lizards of the *anolis* family, which were sometimes so numerous that they might be said to have swarmed there. There were also other lizards of at least three distinct species, but all of them small in size. On the desert plains, at the foot of the hills, the Arizona poisonous lizard was seen; but of this more presently.

Snakes also abounded in some of these little parks, being apparently attracted by the number of lizards, on which they prey. A snake was seen to dart on a lizard, and begin to gorge it. It was compelled to release its prey, but the lizard was weak, and seemed to be hurt; and though care was taken of it, it died in a few hours: yet the snake was not a poisonous one. It seems as if the gastric juice, or saliva, of some reptiles is poisonous to their victims: can the silly superstition of the venom of toads, etc., have arisen from observation of some such incident as that just mentioned?

It would be interesting to know how it is that the ground of all the Parks, great and small, in this region, is so perfectly flat. I could perceive no reason for it, any more than I could for the fact that the vegetation within the Park always differed from that in the surrounding country. River agency did not seem to have anything to do with it, because the character of the Park was the same whether a stream flowed through it or not. One or two of these Parks were simply recesses in the mountains, there being no way through. One was a great rift in the rocks nearly a mile deep, and with walls 1000 feet high. It gradually dwindled in breadth to a mere crack in which there was but just room for a man to squeeze his body. In this case, the surrounding rocks, although vertical, were ragged and broken; and an active man might, perhaps, have, in a few places, climbed to the plateau above. In the narrowest part of this gorge, several pines which had fallen had become jammed, forming a bridge several hundred feet above the spectator.

Two days' journey west of this spot, and somewhere very close to the territory frontier, we found some remarkable ruins of seemingly ancient Indian origin, but with traces of Spanish handiwork also. These consisted of low, square houses in the Indian style, but of much greater architectural finish than those we, at a subsequent period, met with in the forests of the upper Purus in South America. Some of these houses, or huts (for they were mostly one-storied), had been added to, and altered, by Spanish workmanship; and there seemed to have been a mining village, or station, here formerly. There were traces of horizontal shafts driven into the rocks, but they were all securely blocked. The only one we succeeded in penetrating into scarcely had the appearance of a mine, and I am inclined to think it was intended for a hiding-place.

The entrance to this gallery was partially blocked by débris which had fallen from the rocks above: there was only sufficient room left for a man to crawl in on his hands and knees. We cleared away some of the rubbish, and, furnished with lanterns, explored a considerable portion of the gallery, which was of singular formation. The entrance was 6 feet high, sufficient to permit of men walking upright, though it was a bare 3 feet wide.

The work of cutting this passage through the hard rock must have been immense; and probably it had been effected by forced Indian labour. A hundred yards from the entrance the passage suddenly widened to about 8 feet, but remained only 6 feet high, the rocky walls and roof being hard as granite and perfectly dry. There were several side galleries, driven at right angles to the main one. The air in them was so bad that only one could be explored to the end. It ended abruptly, and we found nothing to indicate for what purpose it had been excavated. It was only 4 feet wide, and nothing whatever was found in it.

Continuing along the main gallery a distance of about 300 yards, we found it slope upwards with a sharp rise, and after proceeding along it another 200 yards, were obliged to stop: for, either on account of want of ventilation, or because the air was vitiated, we could not breathe without extreme difficulty. We could see that the gallery still sloped upwards, and every now and then we passed side borings at distances of 20 to 50 yards from each other.

Two hundred yards from the entrance we found the bones of three human skeletons lying in a heap together; and 60 yards further in was a fourth, lying across a sort of box, or wooden tray, which contained a knife and several small hammers, shaped like picks. This last skeleton was that of a small woman, or girl. The bones did not seem to have been at all disturbed; and tresses of long black hair lay by the skulls, proving that these persons had been of the Indian race. Iron rings were let into the walls at frequent intervals, and from some of them iron chains still dangled; but there was no appearance of the dead having been confined while alive: on the contrary, they had all the appearance of having died where they lay; and the chains were found to be just the width of the gallery, and could be hitched over iron knobs on the opposite wall. They therefore seemed to have been used as a barrier. The presence of these rings and chains is conclusive proof that the Spaniards or some other Europeans had been in this subterranean passage, and used it for some purpose.

A careful examination of the rock in many places failed to show the slightest trace of gold or other metal, and therefore it is impossible to think that this gallery was used for any mining purpose. It was probably a hiding-place and secret store-house; and the peculiar conformation of the passage seemed to be well adapted for defence, and preventing an enemy from smoking out fugitives who might have taken refuge here. The Indian skeletons were probably the remains of some brutal Spanish murder, aboriginal life under the rule of the Don being of no more account than that of vermin.

In several of the houses there were Spanish utensils and articles of furniture, though these had been disturbed by some previous visitor. In one house was a chair which fell to pieces on being handled, for it was thoroughly worm-eaten. Some prints of the Virgin and the Crucifixion, hanging on the walls, were in better preservation; though on one of these some impious cowboy had scrawled his ribald verses, thus leaving evidence that the place had occasional visitors —the reason, probably, that nothing of any value was left behind, if I except some curious pieces of porcelain which I felt justified in appropriating.

From New Mexico I, of course, passed westward into Arizona; but it may be as well to remark here that at the time of my first exploration of this region, I considered, and have termed in a former work, a vastly greater tract as New Mexico, than is now officially known by that designation. It is only after a very careful study of the best modern maps I could procure, and with the assistance of an American friend who thoroughly knows the ground, that I have succeeded in fixing localities to the extent indicated in this book. The map I had with me during this journey was so poor and defective that it was of no more use than a piece of waste paper; but, fortunately, many of the old local names have been retained in modern maps, and this has been of great assistance to me in fixing the locality of places visited. These remarks, perhaps, will explain how some few mistakes, which have been pointed out, occurred in writing the work in question, and dispose the critic to be lenient with me. At the time of making most of the journeys herein sketched I was absolutely ignorant of the political boundaries and circumstances of the majority of the "Eleven Eaglets." For other details of these Western journeys our "Great Forests and Deserts of North America" may be consulted. There is matter therein which we are not at liberty to repeat.

A journey of ten hours through a narrow pass leading over a range of mountains, which I calculated to rise at least 7000 feet above the surrounding country, took us, I believe, from the territory of New Mexico into that of Arizona; but the precise time or spot where the crossing took place I am ignorant of.

The pass had more of the character of a narrow valley than a cañon, the sides sloping up at an angle low enough to admit of their being densely clothed with the finest pine forest I had seen for a very long time, many of the trees being at least 200 feet high. This forest covered an immense area, as I could see from certain of the high points of the pass.

RELCAIMING THE ARID SOUTHWEST

The following article describes the difficulties of cultivation of the land in New Mexico and Arizona along with detailed accounts of irrigation projects and the contributions of various officials.

Source: *Forum*, May 1902, 363-71.

IRRIGATION, with the complementary question of water-storage, is one of the most interesting and vital problems now confronting the citizens of Arizona and New Mexico. The results already achieved in the reclamation of their semi-arid lands are inviting national attention; while the promising future outlook is making possible for these Territories a large increase of immigration, not only on the part of foreigners, but also of home and money seekers from the more thickly settled North and East. A study of this water problem must be prefaced by a review of the more important physical characteristics of that country, so long known as the Great American Desert and as a region given over to Indian troubles, cattle-thieving, and wrangles between herdsmen.

New Mexico and Arizona comprise, respectively, an area of 122,000 and 114,000 square miles. The face of the country is a vast tableland — part of the Colorado plateau — of very considerable elevation, relieved by rugged and detached Rocky Mountain chains in the northerly and easterly portions, with a tendency to slope gradually into sandy and gravelly plains toward the extreme southerly and southwesterly regions. The climate is diverse, ranging from the semi-tropical heat of the southern portions to the invigorating cold of the northerly mountains. During the entire year the sun shines brightly through cloudless skies. The rainfall is slight, rarely exceeding ten inches.

The soil is generally a rich, warm, loose, and loamy earth, which is only waiting for water to make it rival in fertility the Nile Valley and become capable of supporting a dense population. In its virgin state, however, it looks to the Eastern farmer about as promising as a sea beach. In the desert regions there is much alkali land. Grama, mesquite, salt, and buffalo grasses flourish luxuriantly, and afford a rarely failing pasturage for the great herds. In the autumn the uncut grass turns to hay, saving the expense of cutting, baling, and storing.

The census of 1900 records 122,931 people in Arizona and 195,310 in New Mexico, the majority in both instances being of native parents, descendants of Americans and Mexicans, and constituting a permanent resident population. The population includes, however, 12,000 Indians in Arizona and 25,000 in New Mexico, with a few scattered Chinese, Japanese, and negroes. Mining, horticulture, agriculture, and stock raising are the leading pursuits.

Because of the scarcity of the rain and the uncertainty of its fall, together with the remarkable fertility of the soil whenever water is applied, there has been from remote times a desire to gather water from the rivers and other streams, to draw it from its main courses into canals and reservoirs, to use it bountifully in the spring and summer, and to accumulate it plentifully during the few weeks of winter or the rainy season. The cliff dwellers and the ancient Toltecs and Aztecs, like the Assyrians and the Egyptians, practised the arts of irrigation, and well understood the problem of conveying water to the uplands. Even now, in many of the valleys, there can be readily traced the lines of great canals from which the early husbandman watered his corn and beans. When these peoples disappeared irrigation went too, and it has been almost a lost calling until within the last fifteen years.

There are, at this time, some 450,000 acres of irrigable land in the beautiful Salt River Valley of Southern Arizona; and what was once an arid waste is now the loveliest of garden spots — a great territory fifteen miles wide, lying between the Verde and the Gila Rivers, and extending fifty miles along Salt River, the main artery whose numerous canals are the blood-vessels that bring life to the soil. The total flow of the canals approximates 1,000,000 gallons per minute. The main laterals have a length of nearly 400 miles, and the integral mileage is very extensive. Foremost are the Arizona and the Grand Canals. The former is forty-seven miles long, beginning near the junction of the Verde and the Salt Rivers, twenty-eight miles east of Phoenix, skirting the foothills to the north, and rendering fit for horticultural and agricultural purposes a large area of semi-tropical desert. Other great canals, including the Consolidated, irrigate the southern portion of the valley, while carrying the life-giving waters far out over the plains and lavishly distributing their riches. Notable, indeed, is the contrast between the luxuriant irrigated areas and the sage-brush desert above.

In Northeastern Arizona, each of the counties of Navajo and Apache contains over 10,000 acres of reclaimed land. Fully 100,000 more acres of land in Navajo could be reclaimed immediately by means of water storage. Nearly 4,000,000 acres in Mohave County are only waiting to receive the waters of the mighty Colorado as soon as it can be diverted from the deep and tortuous channels through which it runs.

Irrigation can be conducted successfully in many parts of New Mexico. There are already in operation, in the north, the Springer system, with fifty miles of ditches and five reservoirs for 22,000 acres, and the Vermajo, with fifty-seven miles of ditches and ten reservoirs for 30,000 acres. In the northwest there are 200 miles of ditches supplying 24,000 acres, and in the southwest, in Grant County, there is an extensive ditch system. In the central portions over fifty companies have been organized and are only awaiting the necessary capital. In addition, there is the Rio Grande Valley, where, particularly in the vicinity of Santa Fé, from the earliest days there has been irrigation in a small way. This valley, 300 miles long by thirty miles wide, if placed under irrigation, would, it is estimated, support 1,500,000 people.

Undoubtedly the greatest system in the arid Southwest is in the Pecos Valley of Southeastern New Mexico, where over $4,000,000 has been expended by private enterprise during the last twelve years in turning aside the waters of the Pecos River and making a wonderfully exuberant garden of the valley famed in song and story as the former retreat of the most desperate train-robbers, cattle-thieves, and other outlaws that the West has ever known. In this valley, which is one hundred and twenty miles long, two enormous reservoirs, McMillan Lake and Lake Avalon, have been made by the erection of dams carried across the river just north of Carlsbad. One of these is 1,140 feet over the top, and completely fills a notch worn by the river through a bed of solid limestone. McMillan Lake is thirteen miles long, and contains enough water to supply the entire lower valley; while Lake Avalon is half as large. There are now available for cultivation over 250,000 acres, of which perhaps one-fifth is engaged. Here irrigation has not only restored a sun-baked alkali plain, but it has created several prosperous little settlements, and has transformed the towns of Carlsbad and Roswell from uninteresting and shadeless gambling-holes into attractive and lively small cities, each with a wealth of fine trees, hedges, and other physical attributes of the well-ordered New England community.

More than 1,000 miles of canals, main and sub-lateral, carry the waters of the Pecos to a myriad of little farms, where they are sent through tiny ditches, banked with earth, until every living organism has received its share. At the unusually low yearly rate of $1.25 per acre, the farmer has the right, at twenty-four hours' notice, to all he needs. The water is hard and of an excellent quality; but its chief virtue is the possession of a great quantity of carbonates and phosphates. Moreover, the valley is a veritable bed of gushing springs; one of them being sufficient to irrigate 20,000 acres, and another having a flow of 1,000 gallons per minute. Here are grown the finest cantaloupes in existence, as well as peaches, apples, pears, grapes, and plums of the highest standard of excellence. The vegetables arrive early, and include beets, asparagus, sweet and Irish potatoes, cauliflower, onions, cabbages, and celery. The local markets take a large share of these crops, and the remainder finds a quick sale as far north as Minnesota. Much of the land is devoted to alfalfa, Kaffir corn, sorghum, millet, and other forage crops, these being the most profitable because of the large tributary ranches.

Some very large farms are owned by prominent stockmen — men who are not only alive to the value of breeding home-grown Durham and Hereford bulls, Rambouillet and Merino rams, and Berkshire and Poland China boars, instead of importing them from Europe, or from Missouri, Kansas, and Illinois, but who realize the growing demand for home-grown stock throughout the Southwest and in Mexico. Ranchmen are profiting by fattening the range cattle on alfalfa, while the sheep raisers top the Kansas City markets with lambs matured on milo maize.

Probably the finest stock farm in New Mexico is that owned by Major Littlefield. It is situated near Roswell, and contains 1,256 acres, a very small fraction of his total land-holdings. The farm is divided into fields of from twenty to eighty acres each. Sixty-five acres are devoted to apples, of which the crop last year was enormous and of the finest quality. Each field is surrounded by an irrigating ditch six feet in width. Besides choice fruit and vegetables, enough alfalfa is grown to fatten the blooded stock, as well as to tide over any emergency in case the grass should give out on one of the big Littlefield ranches. Additional water is supplied from an artesian well, 580 feet deep and of a six-inch bore, which throws a solid stream thirty-five feet high. The water is fresh and is particularly available during the winter when the ditches occasionally freeze. Bordering one side of the farm is a roadway embowered by graceful cottonwoods and prettily termed "Lover's Lane." Here for three miles the shade is so dense that the skylight at the far end resembles the headlight of a locomotive in the distance.

Irrigation means intensive farming — the maximum yield on the minimum area. While the initial outlay is high, the results more than justify the extra expenditure. In the Pecos Valley land that was originally worth fifty cents an acre now brings twenty dollars an acre; while, to cite another illustration, in the horticultural districts of Southern

Arizona, improved land frequently sells for one hundred dollars an acre and even more. Irrigation means permanency of residence among a class of small landholders, which in turn suggests an increase of population.

Foremost of the crops made possible by irrigation is alfalfa, sometimes called lucerne or Spanish clover, a hardy and aggressive plant which has revolutionized the stock industry, besides affording a prosperous occupation to the small farmer. Alfalfa not only grows rapidly and with little care, but it acts as a fertilizer. In the Salt River Valley alone nearly 100,000 acres are devoted to its culture. To the progressive stockman it is a blessing, for it relieves him of the expense, trouble, and risk from climatic changes incident to sending his yearlings and two-year-old steers to the Middle States to be fattened and matured before shipment to market. Three months in the alfalfa fields will work as many favorable changes in the thin range cattle as one year on Northern fields.

When it is remembered that on the open range twenty acres per year are allowed each head of cattle, and that one acre of alfalfa will support two head, the value of this product will be readily perceived. Again, if we take the appraised value of government land, one dollar the acre, and add to this two and one-half dollars as the minimum cost of making it irrigable, we find that by spending upon it two and one-half times its commercial worth as unreclaimed land its value will, through irrigation, appreciate forty-fold.

Alfalfa, too, is responsible for the continued prosperity in the hog business, though it is to the climate that the entire absence of cholera is due. Both in cheapness and efficacy as a flesh-builder alfalfa is better than corn. A steady and profitable market for Arizona hogs has been opened in Southern California, while from places much farther away is coming an appreciable demand for "alfalfa pork."

Until recently, the breeding of horses has not been considered in the light of an industry in the Southwest, for the reason that the hardy little cow-pony, as prolific as any prairie weed, supplied all demands. Now there is a call from the towns and mining districts for a larger and stockier animal, and breeders are achieving favorable results in the alfalfa pastures.

Two other profitable though widely divergent activities following the promotion of alfalfa culture are bee-keeping and ostrich-farming; the former now yielding annually over one million pounds in Arizona alone. Chicago is the principal market, and the output is largely used by confectioners and bakers. Ostrich raising is of comparatively recent date, but results have proved highly encouraging. In Southern Arizona there are several companies and considerably over one thousand ostriches. The climate is as conducive to the plumed giants as that of South Africa; and they thrive amazingly well on the rich alfalfa, requiring no shelter and but little care, besides yielding a substantial plucking once every eight months.

Of the cereals grown, barley, corn, and wheat are the most common. The two former are cut in the straw and fed to stock. In both Territories, particularly in the towns and mining settlements, there is an increasing demand for wheat, and home industry is further encouraged by the high prices of Eastern and Northern flour.

The raising of the sugar-beet promises to develop into a leading industry. Sugar factories have been started in both Territories, the largest being in Carlsbad, New Mexico, where nearly 2,000 acres are devoted to beet culture.

Watermelons, muskmelons, strawberries, blackberries, and all kinds of vegetables are staple products, and vie with the finest varieties of the East. As no finer climate exists for the propagation of grapes, viticulturists have enjoyed a large measure of the prevailing fertility of the reclaimed lands. The grapes, with and without seeds, are heavy in saccharine, and include such vinous favorites as the Mission, which was brought into New Mexico early in the eighteenth century by the Catholic missionaries, the Muscat, the Hamburg, the Malvoisie, and others.

Other horticultural possibilities, notably in the warmer portions, include date-palms, almonds, nectarines, olives, apricots, figs, oranges, and lemons. Several hundred date-palm trees have been successfully raised at the experimental station near Phœnix, Arizona, and flourish as they did of old in Algiers, Egypt, and Arabia. Almond trees yield plenteously, but, like the lemon, they are susceptible to the spring frosts. Apricots ripen early in May, nearly a month in advance of the California fruit. Figs grow profusely, but the market is too distant for them to be shipped fresh. In the Salt River Valley oranges and lemons of a superior quality are raised in abundance. In common with other Arizona fruits, they are exempt from the scale insect, and present a bright and wholesome appearance, being much sought after in the large cities.

If irrigation did nothing more than to encourage the growth of shade trees, hedges, and shrubbery in the Southwestern towns, its service would still be great. Much interest has been taken, particularly in Southern Arizona, in beautifying the streets and parks with the foliage of two zones. The visitor sees a pleasing arrangement of the stately ash and cottonwood, the dreamy pepper, the lofty date-palm, the locust, and the desert willow, besides quantities of dwarf palms and rose-bushes.

Though the present scheme of irrigation rests on a sound basis, it is still little more than a beginning. All available water not in actual use should be stored; and for this purpose there is need of many dams and reservoirs, with which to increase the water supply in those canals which now carry a deficient volume in the dry season, as well as to provide a sufficiently large and constant supply enabling the restoration of further areas of arid wastes to be proceeded with. Upon the storage of the flood waters depends to a very large extent the future development of agriculture in both Territories.

Throughout Arizona and New Mexico there are many natural storage sites to absorb the regular drain of the mountains, and already several important projects have been started to erect the necessary dams. On the Gila River of Arizona, at a point called The Buttes, fourteen miles from Florence, a dam 150 feet high will store enough water to cover 174,000 acres to a depth of one foot, or, in other words, will impound 174,000 acre-feet. At Riverside, a dam of the same dimensions will impound still more; while at San Carlos, on the Apache Reservation, is a site for a reservoir easily capable of impounding 361,000 acre-feet. The so-called Horseshoe Reservoir, on the Rio Verde, has an estimated capacity of 204,935 acre-feet, sufficient to irrigate 50,000 acres. It is taking nearly $1,000,000 to construct the Agua Fria River system. The canal will be thirty miles long and forty-five feet in width, and the estimated area that will be irrigated is 150,000 acres. The grandest scheme yet devised is the Tonto Basin project in Salt River Valley, sixty miles northeast of Phœnix, where it is purposed, at an expense of $2,500,000, to dam a gorge in the cañon of Salt River and form an artificial lake of eighteen square miles. Into this basin will be carried the "run off" from a drainage area of 6,000 square miles, most of which is in the region of greatest precipitation in Arizona. The capacity will only be limited by the height of the dam; but the amount planned is 757,000 acre-feet. About 300,000 acres will thus become fit for cultivation.

Good sites are obtainable in the four corners of New Mexico, notably the Canadian River country in the northeast, the Pecos Valley in the southeast, the Gila and the Colorado River in the west, the San Juan River in the northwest, and also throughout the Rio Grande Valley from El Paso to the Colorado line. It is stated that the flood-waters from the great watershed of the White Mountains in Eastern New Mexico are sufficient to irrigate 1,500,000 acres.

The question of the public and private control of irrigation is exciting great attention just now, particularly among the citizens of the respective Territories, who see in the present great development of private systems an argument not only for Statehood, but also for public control and management. Mr. Vernon L. Clark, Immigration Commissioner for Maricopa County, Arizona, writing on November 29, 1901, said:

> I believe that the admission of this Territory to Statehood will have much to do with the future development of irrigation in Arizona, and *vice versa*. We have, in this Territory, many millions of acres of the most fertile land in the world, providing we can get water upon it. In the point of State control or the handling by private enterprise of the irrigation systems there seems to be little choice. We have room here for the accommodation of many millions more people, if we can find ways and means of storing the immense volume of water that goes to waste each spring. Not only is the storage of water of immense value to the agricultural country, but it will mean much to the future development of the mining industry. There are hundreds and thousands of rich prospects and mines in Arizona and New Mexico which are now idle because of the lack of water. With water storage we can give a perpetual supply to these mines.

Mr. Laurence H. Hamilton, Secretary of the Phoenix and Maricopa County Board of Trade, writing on November 12, 1901, said:

> Extended irrigation will certainly be an argument in favor of admitting Arizona to Statehood. With Arizona a State, there should be little difficulty in securing government aid in building reservoirs and the consequent reclamation of millions of acres of land. It is my private opinion that government control of irrigation would be profitable and satisfactory. There is, however, at present, a difference of opinion on that point.

Governor Miguel A. Otero, of New Mexico, who is one of the most enthusiastic advocates of Statehood, said, in a letter dated November 5, 1901:

> New Mexico, of course, is very much interested in the subject of irrigation, and we believe that Congress should do something for the arid West in order to reclaim our land. As a Territory, we feel that we can do little in this direction; and this is one of the arguments that we have advanced for speedy admission.

What has been done by private enterprise in reclaiming the mesas and the semi-arid wastes is but a slight indication of what could be done by public control, either national or Territorial. It is suggested that Congress should build reservoirs in the more promising districts and charge a minimum water-rent. No doubt, in some instances, this might be practical, though it would hardly be a safe precedent to establish. It might be successful in the Gila Reservation in Arizona, where over 200,000 of the 350,000 acres could be easily made irrigable, affording an unfailing future support for the 4,000 Indians and for a large white settler population besides. Still better, the national Government might place the reclamation of its lands under the United States Geological Survey, subject to Civil Service control, and authorize that body to proceed with the reclamation of the public domain, and, as soon as a given area was reclaimed, to sell it to settlers. With the revenue thus acquired it would have sufficient means to continue its labor without any further aid from Congress. Again, the Government might cede the arid lands to the Territories in which they lie, so that the question of disposition and development might be one of local legislation. In connection with this suggestion may be cited the views of Governor N. O. Murphy of Arizona, in his annual report for 1901:

Unless it be assumed at the outset that the people are incapable of self-government, there can be no argument whatever against permitting them to take over the public domain and use it as a basis for obtaining capital for the construction of reservoirs. The entire opposition to the suggestion lies in the assumption that the people are essentially corrupt, and that the lawmakers whom they would direct to represent them would be perversely dishonest; in the assumption that it would be impossible for Congress to devise a measure which would properly protect the people from spoliation; and, finally, in the assumption that capital is always dishonest and should have no consideration or encouragement. Happily, such inferential arguments are confined to but a few, and have little popularity in Arizona.

In no part of our country has permanent wealth been created more rapidly than in the reclaimed portions. Thanks to irrigation, the Southwest is beginning to receive a tiny share of that vast tide of immigration which for so many years has flowed into Chicago only to drift toward the Northwest. With the powerful inducements now offered, it behooves the boards of trade, the various corporations, and, most of all, the two great railroad systems to make every possible attempt to attract foreigners to these Territories, besides showing to the men of the North and the East, to men of large means as well as to men of small means, including that great number of people who by reason of weak lungs and otherwise poor health cannot put forth their best efforts in the places where they are now living, the wonderful possibilities of this blossoming desert, where the sun is ever smiling and the rays are tempered by a dry and invigorating atmosphere.   ROBERT M. BARKER.

BASIC FACTS

Capital City	Santa Fe
Nickname	The Land of Enchantment
Flower	Yucca
Bird	Roadrunner
Tree	Piñon
Songs	*Así es Nuevo Mejico* *O, Fair New Mexico*
Gem	Turquoise
Animal	Black Bear
Fish	Cutthroat Trout
Entered the Union	January 6, 1912

STATISTICS*

Land Area (square miles)	121,412
Rank in Nation	5th
Population†	1,076,000
Rank in Nation	37th
Density per square mile	8.9
Number of Representatives in Congress	2
Capital City	Santa Fe
Population	41,167
Rank in State	2nd
Largest City	Albuquerque
Population	243,751
Number of Cities over 10,000 Population	12
Number of Counties	32

---

* Based on 1970 census statistics compiled by the Bureau of the Census.
† Estimated by Bureau of the Census for July 1, 1972.

DOCUMENTS

MAP OF CONGRESSIONAL DISTRICTS
OF NEW MEXICO

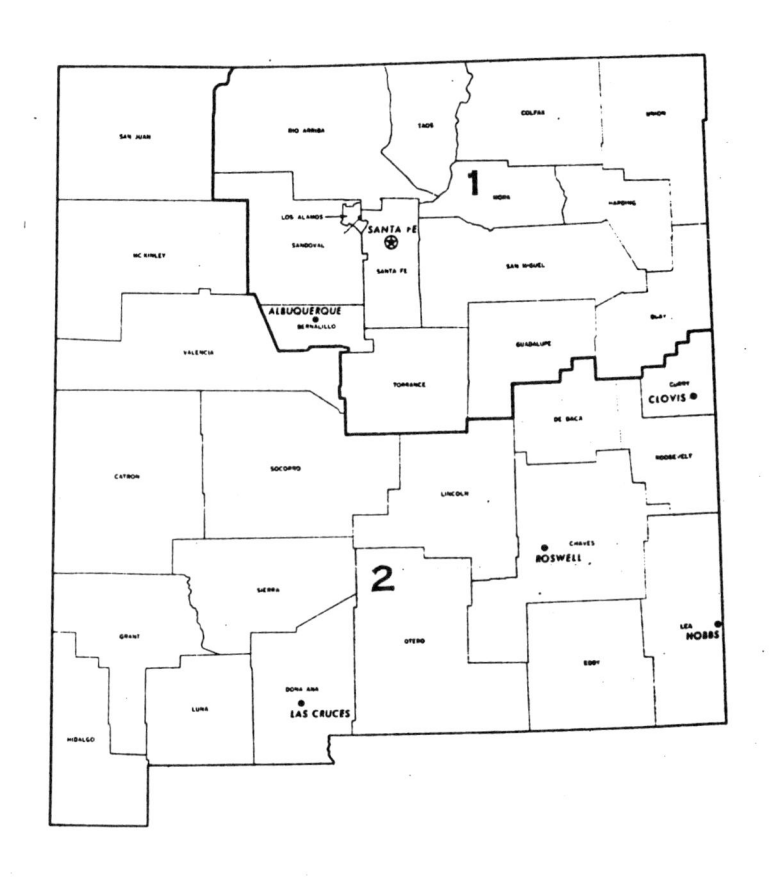

SELECTED BIBLIOGRAPHY

Armstrong, Ruth W. *New Mexico From Arrowhead to Atom.* South Brunswick and New York: A. S. Barnes and Company, 1976.

Arnold, Elliot. *The Time of the Gringo.* New York: Alfred A. Knopf, 1953.

Fergusson, Edna. *New Mexico. A Pageant of Three Peoples.* New York: Alfred A. Knopf, 1964.

Fugate, Francis L. *The Spanish Heritage of the Southwest.* New York: Rinehart and Co., 1951.

An Illustrated History of New Mexico. . . . Chicago: The Lewis Publishing Company, 1895.

Keleher, William A. *Turmoil in New Mexico, 1846-1868.* Santa Fe, New Mexico: The Rydal Prsss, 1952.

Larson, Robert W. *New Mexico Populism. A Study of Radical Protest in a Western Territory.* Boulder, Colo.: Colorado Associated University Press, 1974.

Mann, E. B. and Harvey, Fred E. *New Mexico: Land of Enchantment.* East Lansing: Michigan State University Press, 1955.

Otero, Nina. *Old Spain in Our Southwest.* New York: Harcourt, Brace and Company, 1936.

Peattie, Elia. *The Pictorial Story of America Containing the Romantic Incidents of History.* Chicago: National Publishing Company, 1896.

Wallis, George A. *Cattle Kings of the Staked Plains.* Dallas: American Guild Press, 1957.

Wellman, Paul I. *Glory, God, and Gold, A Narrative History.* Garden City: Doubleday & Co., 1954.

NAME INDEX

Abreu, Santiago, 4
Alarid, Juan Bautista Vigil y, 6
Ana, Col., 8
Ana, Dona, 8
Anderson, Clinton P., 21
Apodaca, Jerry, 23
Armijo, Manuel, 4, 5
Asny, W. E. M., 11
Axtell, Samuel B., 13

Baca, Ezequiel Cabeza
Becknell, William, 4
Baylor, John Robert, 10
Bent, Charles, 6
Billy the Kid, 14
Bolack, Tom, 22
Bonille, Francisco Levya de, 1
Burroughs, John, 22

Calhoun, James S., 7
Campbell, Jack M., 22
Canby, Edward R. S., 10
Cargo, Dabid F., 23
Carleton, James H., 11
Castillo, Sr., 1
Castillo, Bernal Diaz de, 8
Catron, Thomas Benton, 19
Chaves, Mariano, 14
Chavez, Francisco Javier, 4
Chavez, Jose Antonio, 4
Chavez, Mariano, 5
Chumuscado, Francisco, 1
Colfax, Schuyler, 12
Connelly, Henry, 10
Cooke, Philip St. George, 9
Coronado, Francisco Vasquez, 1
Cortez, Hernando, 8
Cruzate, Domingo Jironza Petriz de, 3
Cubero, Don Pedro, 3
Curry, George, 16

Dillon, Richard C., 20
Doruntes, 1

Eddy, Charles B., 14
Elkins, Stephen B., 13
Espejo, Antonio, 1
Esteban, a slave, 1
Ewell, Richard S., 9

Garrett, Pat, 14
Gidding, Marsh, 12
Gonzalez, Jose, 5
Goodnight, Charles, 11
Grant, Ulysses Simpson, 11
Greiner, John, 8

Hagerman, Herbert J., 16
Hannett, Arthur T., 19
Harding, William Gamaliel, 19
Hinley, James J., 19
Hockenhull, Andrew W., 20
Horrell (Harrold or Howell) brothers, 12
Humana, Antonio Gutierrez de, 1

Jicarilla, 8
John the Baptist, Saint, 14

Kearney, Stephen W., 6
Kennedy, John F., 22
King, Bruce, 23

Lamy, Bishop Jean Baptiste, 7, 8
Lane, William Carr, 8
Larrazola, Octaviano A., 18, 19
Lea, Joseph C., 18
Lejanza, Marian Martinez de, 6
Lincoln, Abraham, 12
Lindsey, Washington E., 18
Loring, Oliver, 11
Lynde, Isaac, 10

147

Mabry, Thomas J., 21
Martinez, Paddy, 21
McDonald, William C., 17
McKinley, William, 14, 15
McSween, Alexander, 13
Mechem, Edwin L., 21, 22
Mechem, Merritt C., 19
Mendizabel, Bernardo Lopez de, 2
Meriwether, David, 9
Michael, Saint, 8
Miles, John E., 20
Mills, William J., 17
Mitchell, Robert B., 11

Nurbara, Antonio, 4
Nuroe, John, 7

Onate, Juan de, 1
Ortiz, Juan Rafael, 5
Otermin, Governor, 3
Otero, Miguel Antonio, 15

Pacheco, Alonso, 2
Penalosa, Don Diego de, 2
Perez, Albino, 5
Pershing, John J., 17
Pierce, Franklin, 8
Pile, William A., 12
Prince, L. Bradford, 14

Quay, Matthew Stanley, 16

Renalta Don Pedro de, 2
Rencher, Abraham, 9
Reynolds, J. W., 16
Ritch, William G., 13
Rodriguez, Fray Augustin, 1
Roosevelt, Theodore, 16
Rosas, Luis de, 2
Ross, Edmund G., 14

Sandova, Antonio, 5
Sarracino, Francisco, 5
Seligman, Arthur, 20
Sheldon, Lionel A., 13
Sherman, General, 12
Sibley, H. H., 10, 11
Simms, John F., 21
Sotelo, Felipe de, 1
Summer, E. V., 8

Taft, William Howard, 17
Thornton, William T., 15
Tingley, Clyde, 20
Torrance, Francis, 16

Vaca, Cabeza de, 1
Vargas, Don Diego de, 3
Vigil, Donancoano, 6
Villa, Pancho, 17
Vizcarra, Antonio, 4

Wallace, Lewis, 13
Washington, John Marshall, 6
Wilson, Woodrow, 18

Zaldivar, Juan de, 1